The Happy Prince

33 1/3 Global

33 1/3 Global, a series related to but independent from **33 1/3**, takes the format of the original series of short, music-based books and brings the focus to music throughout the world. With initial volumes focusing on Japanese and Brazilian music, the series will also include volumes on the popular music of Australia/Oceania, Europe, Africa, the Middle East, and more.

33 1/3 Japan

Series Editor: Noriko Manabe

Spanning a range of artists and genres – from the 1970s rock of Happy End to technopop band Yellow Magic Orchestra, the Shibuya-kei of Cornelius, classic anime series *Cowboy Bebop,* J-Pop/EDM hybrid Perfume, and vocaloid star Hatsune Miku – 33 1/3 Japan is a series devoted to in-depth examination of Japanese popular music of the twentieth and twenty-first centuries.

Published Titles:

Supercell's *Supercell* by Keisuke Yamada

AKB48 by Patrick W. Galbraith and Jason G. Karlin

Yoko Kanno's *Cowboy Bebop Soundtrack* by Rose Bridges

Perfume's *Game* by Patrick St. Michel

Cornelius's *Fantasma* by Martin Roberts

Joe Hisaishi's *My Neighbor Totoro: Soundtrack* by Kunio Hara

Shonen Knife's *Happy Hour* by Brooke McCorkle

Nenes's *Koza Dabasa* by Henry Johnson

Yuming's *The 14th Moon* by Lasse Lehtonen

Toshiko Akiyoshi-Lew Tabackin Big Band's *Kogun* by E. Taylor Atkins

S.O.B.'s *Don't Be Swindle* by Mahon Murphy and Ran Zwigenberg

Forthcoming Titles:

Kohaku Utagassen: The Red and White Song Contest by Shelley Brunt

Yellow Magic Orchestra's *Yellow Magic Orchestra* by Toshiyuki Ohwada

33 1/3 Brazil

Series Editor: Jason Stanyek

Covering the genres of samba, tropicália, rock, hip hop, forró, bossa nova, heavy metal and funk, among others, 33 1/3 Brazil is a series devoted to in-depth examination of the most important Brazilian albums of the twentieth and twenty-first centuries.

Published Titles:

Caetano Veloso's *A Foreign Sound* by Barbara Browning

Tim Maia's *Tim Maia Racional Vols. 1 &2* by Allen Thayer

João Gilberto and Stan Getz's *Getz/Gilberto* by Brian McCann

Gilberto Gil's *Refazenda* by Marc A. Hertzman

Dona Ivone Lara's *Sorriso Negro* by Mila Burns

Milton Nascimento and Lô Borges's *The Corner Club* by Jonathon Grasse

Racionais MCs' *Sobrevivendo no Inferno* by Derek Pardue

Naná Vasconcelos's *Saudades* by Daniel B. Sharp

Chico Buarque's First *Chico Buarque* by Charles A. Perrone

Forthcoming Titles:

Jorge Ben Jor's *África Brasil* by Frederick J. Moehn

33 1/3 Europe

Series Editor: Fabian Holt

Spanning a range of artists and genres, 33 1/3 Europe offers engaging accounts of popular and culturally significant albums of Continental Europe and the North Atlantic from the twentieth and twenty-first centuries.

Published Titles:

Darkthrone's *A Blaze in the Northern Sky* by Ross Hagen

Ivo Papazov's *Balkanology* by Carol Silverman

Heiner Müller and Heiner Goebbels's *Wolokolamsker Chaussee* by Philip V. Bohlman

33 1/3 Oceania

Series Editors: Jon Stratton (senior editor) and Jon Dale (specializing in books on albums from Aotearoa/New Zealand)

Spanning a range of artists and genres from Australian Indigenous artists to Maori and Pasifika artists, from Aotearoa/New Zealand noise music to Australian rock, and including music from Papua and other Pacific islands, 33 1/3 Oceania offers exciting accounts of albums that illustrate the wide range of music made in the Oceania region.

Kate Ceberano's *Brave* by Panizza Allmark
Dinah Lee's *Introducing Dinah Lee* by Kimberly Cannady
The Waifs' *Up All Night* by Rebecca Bennison
The Three Out's *Move* by James Gaunt
Split Enz' *Mental Notes* by Michael Lamb
Douglas Lilburn's *Complete Electro-Acoustic Works* by Bruce Russell
Savage Garden's *Affirmation* by Pat O'Grady
Dick Diver's *Calendar Days* by Mitch Ryan
Blood Duster's *Fisting the Dead* by Rosemary Overell
Olivia Newton-John's *Physical* by Jarrod Sturnieks
Stella Donnelly's *Beware of the Dogs* by Emily Wilson

33 1/3 South Asia

Series Editor: Natalie Sarrazin

From the films of Bollywood and Lollywood, to home-grown *bhangra* hip-hop, Hindu devotional pop and Sufi rock, Sri Lankan rap, Indo jazz and disco, new-wave electronica and diasporic Asian Underground scene, 33 1/3 South Asia takes readers on a sonically diverse journey through the most significant soundtracks and albums from the twentieth and twenty-first centuries.

Published Titles:
Dil Chahta Hai Soundtrack by Jayson Beaster-Jones
Lata Mangeshkar's *My Favourites, Volume 2* by Anirudha Bhattacharjee and Chandrashekhar Rao
Coke Studio (Season 14) by Rakae Rehman Jamil and Khadija Muzaffar

33 1/3 Africa

Series Editor: Michael Veal

33 1/3 Africa is a series of books on canonical, album-length works of African music including traditional music, experimental music, and, with particular emphasis, popular music. Academic and journalistic writing results in sophisticated, nuanced and accessible narratives on African music.

Published Titles:

Fela Anikulapo-Kuti's *Sorrow Tears and Blood* by Stephanie Shonekan

Forthcoming Titles:

Cesária Évora's *Miss Perfumado* by Jacqueline Georgis

Paul Simon's *Graceland* by Kalvin Schmidt-Rimpler Dinh

Nico, Rochereau, Roger & L'African Fiesta – *Volume 1 (1962–1963)* by Frank Gunderson

The Happy Prince

John Tebbutt

Series Editor: Jon Stratton, UniSA Creative, University of South
Australia, and Jon Dale, University of Melbourne, Australia

BLOOMSBURY ACADEMIC
NEW YORK • LONDON • OXFORD • NEW DELHI • SYDNEY

BLOOMSBURY ACADEMIC
Bloomsbury Publishing Inc, 1359 Broadway, New York, NY 10018, USA
Bloomsbury Publishing Plc, 50 Bedford Square, London, WC1B 3DP, UK
Bloomsbury Publishing Ireland, 29 Earlsfort Terrace, Dublin 2, D02 AY28, Ireland

BLOOMSBURY, BLOOMSBURY ACADEMIC and the Diana logo
are trademarks of Bloomsbury Publishing Plc

First published in the United States of America 2026

Bloomsbury Publishing Inc does not have any control over, or responsibility
for, any third-party websites referred to or in this book. All internet addresses
given in this book were correct at the time of going to press. The author and
publisher regret any inconvenience caused if addresses have changed or sites
have ceased to exist, but can accept no responsibility for any such changes.

A catalog record for this book is available from the Library of Congress.

ISBN: HB: 979-8-7651-1404-9
          PB: 979-8-7651-1403-2
          ePDF: 979-8-7651-1406-3
          eBook: 979-8-7651-1405-6

Series: 33 1/3 Oceania

Typeset by Integra Software Services Pvt. Ltd.
Printed and bound in the United States of America

For product safety related questions contact productsafety@bloomsbury.com.

To find out more about our authors and books visit www.bloomsbury.com
and sign up for our newsletters.

Contents

Figures

Acknowledgements

Projects such as this are collaborative and I have had good fortune in that many people have given time and other assistance. The reference section has a full list of interviews, but I want to thank the remaining band members, Kevin Borich and Brett Nielsen, for their willingness to go back sixty years to tell me their story. Bobi Petch (nee Nicholas) was the key that unlocked so much information. She is not only knowledgeable but good natured and generous. For my part I want to thank my family of readers, particularly Lyn Berends and Luke Tebbutt. Their insights were indispensable. My editor Jon Dale has been a rock. His early support and ongoing encouragement have been crucial in getting me here. A special thanks to Bic Runga for permission to quote lyrics from 'Beautiful Collision' in the introduction.

For resources and assistance, special thanks are due to Christine Mintrom and Melanie and Dennis Winters. Jaesen Jones shared unpublished research on the recording of the album. The Alexander Turnbull Library, Wellington, and the Australian Defence Force Academy Research Library, Canberra, provided access to important records. Glenn A. Baker passed on a crucial contact at an opportune time. Magic. Thanks also to Doug Ashdown, Graeme Brown, Peter Cox, Peter Doyle, Robert Drummond, Brian Ferrier, Catherine Dwyer (National Film and Sound Archives), Roger Foley-Fogg, Les Gock, Shane Hewitt, Dom Hofstede, John Kenny, David Lillicott, Hugh Liney, Ed Matzenik, David Nichols, David

Pepperall, Peter Russell (Flynns Beach Books and Records), Noel Sanders, Lorraine Sainsbury, Ted Spring, Susan Thomas (Special Collections Assistant Curator, ADFA/UNSW Library), Phillip Virgo (Colour Factory), Geoffrey Walden, John Widmer and David Williams.

Introduction

Do you know what it means
To abandon your dreams
To leave with the storms rolling by
How the clouds on this day
Come to take you away
'Til you're gone, gone
Far away from me

Bic Runga, 'Beautiful Collision'

Few people now will have heard the La De Da's, *The Happy Prince*.[1] It was released in 1969 as a vinyl LP in Australia and New Zealand. Later, the complete album was included in a compilation of the band's recordings, *The La De Das – Rock'N'Roll Decade 1964–'74*, (1981), which was released as 2 LP's and on cassette. A bowdlerized CD that included versions with and without narratiion, was produced in New Zealand in 2005 but it has not been released since. That it exists at all results from a 'beautiful collision' between musical camaraderie and a catalytic, hippie enthusiasm – a romance if you like, nourished by a serendipitous universe.

The La De Da's had long dreamt of recording this album. They believed it would establish a place for them in international contemporary music, but they needed a producer and a studio that could realize their vision for *The Happy Prince* – a rendering of Oscar Wilde's story into a contemporary musical idiom. The band were tight – musically and personally – and recording the album had become a passion project: they wanted to make an artistic statement that was informed by the shift in music towards albums as complete entities. The band's proposed third album would be their first with all original material and it had also become a measure of their success. They believed their ideal production could bring international recognition beyond Oceania, in London, their pop mecca. The La De Da's had nurtured this ambition for over a year and they thought they had found a producer in Irish 'ex-pat' producer Jim Stewart.

Stewart was in the throes of establishing a new label, Sweet Peach. He had gained a reputation for innovative production with an Australian psychedelic Top 10 hit in May 1968, 'The Love Machine', by Pastoral Symphony. Working independently to produce and record 'The Love Machine', Stewart had put together a studio band – the first such approach to production in Australia – and worked with gun engineer Roger Savage to create an innovative phased sound for the track. At the end of 1968 Stewart was working at Gamba in Adelaide. The studio was funded by Derek Jolly, heir to the Penfold wine fortune. Established in 1966, Gamba had a reputation for being well-equipped, with both a hands-off, 'let the artists work' ethic and a first-class sound (Jolly imported the first Moog synthesizer into Australia for Gamba in 1969). The band had tried other studios in Australia over the last eighteen months but had yet to produce a record. This contrasted with their earlier production history in New Zealand, where they had put down two albums and released half a dozen hit singles in the two years since they turned professional at the end of 1965. These disastrous Australian studio experiences have become mythical. In November 1968 that was all supposed to change. Only it didn't.

On Thursday, 14 November, the band were in Melbourne for gigs and to begin preparing for their studio date in Adelaide, another nine hours' drive south-west of Melbourne. Set up in a rehearsal room, they began working on arrangements for the session. One of their most ardent supporters, hippie bon vivant and raconteur, Adrian Rawlins, sat in. Rawlins, a music journalist and performance poet, had recently emerged from a self-imposed seclusion to engage with Australia's burgeoning pop/rock/psychedelic music scene. An adherent of Meher Baba (the laughing guru), Rawlins was an enthusiastic publicist who was happy to tell people about the La De Da's: 'The minute I heard them I recognised a very rare creativity in their playing' (Rawlins, 1969). Rawlins left the sessions after an hour or so and it seemed to him that the band's professionalism had set them up for a productive recording session the following week, but five days later, by Tuesday, the session was off.

The reasons were confused. One news report had it that the studio was just not ready for the band. Another claimed the studio had been demolished. Historically, the abandoned Gamba sessions rarely rate a footnote in the band's biographies.[2] A contemporary report in *Go Set* (1968), Australia's national youth newspaper, had it that the band 'had packed their bags, loaded the vans and were ready to go' when they rang to confirm the address of the studio, only to find the session had been abandoned. *Go Set* reported that the band had, as a result, decided 'not record at all in Australia [but to] wait till [*sic*] they get to England to cut any records' (1968). The lure of an international career had always been a motivator for the New Zealand band. They saw Australia as a necessary step to get to a larger scene in London, one they had only previously experienced through listening to recordings on the BBC World Service.

Instead of the planned time in the studio, the band retreated from Melbourne to a regional location and worked up their songs before a twelve-hour drive back to Sydney for December performances. Rawlins happened to be travelling through Sydney at the same time, on his way farther north to Queensland, when he met up with the band again. While it appeared that the Adelaide disappointment would be the last word on recording *The Happy Prince* in Australia, 'fate knew otherwise', according to Rawlins: '[A]fter hearing them at a leading disco, Here [in North Sydney], I urged them to continue with the idea of recording *The Happy Prince*' (Rawlins 1969). As a result, Bruce Howard, the band's keyboard player and musical leader, spoke to their publishing company, Essex, who agreed to support the band and approached EMI Sydney on their behalf. The final shoe dropped when the band's booking agent and ersatz manager (the La De Da's never had an official manager), Harry Widmer of Cordon Bleu, agreed to pay for sessions at EMI's 301 Studio in Castlereagh St, Sydney. By January 1969, the band had begun four weeks of recording with EMI's house producer David Woodley-Page.

The album was finally released to critical acclaim in June that year. The La De Da's were, however, still intent on taking the product to England and left Australia soon after its release. Without a tour or promotion locally, the album soon disappeared from public view. *The Happy Prince* languished on the periphery of Australian music, known largely only to collectors and cognoscenti. Unsurprisingly, then, my own introduction to *The Happy Prince* was circuitous. It initially came by way of historical research into Melbourne as a music city (Homan et al. 2021). Our project found that the Fat Black Pussycat, a small club in the well-to-do suburb of Toorak, had held jazz and poetry evenings in the early 1960s curated by Adrian Rawlins. That fact did not make it into our book, but I became fascinated with Rawlins's relationship to Australian music. Not long after, I was visiting Flynns Beach Book and Record Shop in Port Macquarie, north of Sydney, when I came across an album. The cover was familiar although I had not seen it before. It turned out that it was painted by Bob Haberfield, who produced the cover art for Michael Moorcock books published in the popular Mayflower Science Fantasy paperback series, quite a few of which I had read. On the back cover it was revealed that the narrator was Adrian Rawlins! Narrator? The lyric sheet told me the LP was based on an original story by Oscar Wilde. Wilde, Rawlins, Moorcock and the La De Da's. It was *The Happy Prince* and I had to have it.

I had known of the La De Da's as a 1970s blues-rock outfit, but this did not prepare me for the experience of listening to *The Happy Prince*. Now, I concur with Martin Delia, who, in his Aussie Music Blog, wrote of the La De Da's: 'They're practically the only major group (on either shore [New Zealand/Australia]) to emerge from the beat boom of 1964–65 who managed to ride out the massive musical changes of the Sixties and adapt to the new scene in the Seventies.' This album was pivotal in that journey. It is a measure of how success sustains popular music histories that *The Happy Prince* had largely disappeared from popular view. This book brings an important pop text back to the light.

Haberfield's album cover drew me in even before I listened to the album. (For more on album art in Australia see **https://bloomsbury.pub/the-happy-prince/album-art**). It opened a window to the band's journey from the 1960s Auckland beat scene to Sydney psychedelia. The titles were in psychedelic typography of the era. They harked back to an *art nouveaux* past while the air-brushed images soared into an unknown future, capturing the flight of The Swallow and the eponymous Prince, the protagonists in Wilde's story. The album opens with Adrian Rawlins's narration. His plummy, theatrical camp sat me up; this was not going to be an ordinary listening experience. The album is, in fact, a unique adaptation of literary text. I suggest that it is the ultimate 'cover' – not just a song but a whole classic text! Like sampling now cover songs in the 1960s were a form of *homage*. A way to let listeners in on other musicians that a band was digging. At a time when the whole idea of albums was a fluid conception, the La De Da's looked to steal the march internationally on what a 'cover' could be. And in the process contributed to a then novel idea – a concept album. Who came first is, I suggest, more a pea-and-thimble exercise than a historical question and in the end, what really matters for me – and I hope to you dear readers – is that the La De Da's produced an original contribution to pop music with *The Happy Prince*.

1 La De Da's

Introduction

In their initial years from 1964 to 1967 the La De Da's were a Tāmaki Makaurau/Auckland band – a rocking top forty hit machine in their home country of Aotearoa/New Zealand – and 1966 was their breakout year, when they released an eponymous debut album and three singles. Two years later, they had moved 'across the ditch' to Sydney, becoming the psychedelic 'disco gods' of Australia's east coast and producing their acclaimed third album *The Happy Prince* (1969). Then they morphed once again into a blues-rock power trio before they disappeared, disbanding in 1975. This book traces the trajectory of the band with a focus on *The Happy Prince* considered by many as New Zealand and Australia's first concept album.

The band began as The Mergers in 1963, when school friends at Te Atatū's Rutherford High School – Kevin Borich (b.1948 guitar), Brett Nielsen (b.1947 drums) and Trevor Wilson (b.1949–d.2009 bass) – came together to play instrumentals, *a la* The Shadows, for local dances. Within a year Phil Key (b.1949–d.1984) signed on as rhythm guitarist and singer and they became the La De Da's. Later Bruce Howard (b.1948–d.2021) joined them on keyboards to complete the line-up. By 1965, they had produced their first single and, in two years, had two LPs and numerous hits in New Zealand, including the first local No. 1 – it famously took top spot from The Beatles – in that country's National Hit Parade. They built a relationship with the Stebbing family's studio in Auckland, before eventually settling in Australia and becoming a successful performance band in Sydney and Melbourne. Chart success came much later in Australia, by which time the band had lost three of its early, influential members. This chapter follows the La De Da's in their early days from the mid-1960s, a time when the band was learning their craft and experimenting musically, experiences that eventually fed into *The Happy Prince*, their first Australian long player. The chapter also introduces Auckland, a city that was newly riven by motorways, in particular the Northwestern Motorway, which linked the primarily rural west with the heart of the city. This was not the open road you might usually associate with rock music. It was more a sinew: a tightly wrought ribbon of tarmac, not so much subject to a wind of freedom but the whiff of dissolution, change, a reckoning of identities built on top of already existing lives.

The La De Da's emerge

The La De Da's came together through accident and coincidence. The nucleus was formed between 1962 and 1963 when schoolboys Kevin Borich, Brett Nielsen and Trevor Wilson met at one of Auckland's newest schools, Rutherford High School, and formed The Mergers. Phil Key joined the group in late 1963, and not long after, the band's name changed to the La De Da's. Bruce Howard approached the band after seeing them play in 1965. Rutherford, however, was an important starting point. The school began taking students in February 1961 and soon developed a reputation for its disciplinarian approach. Catering to the burgeoning population in Auckland's northwest, it provided a crucial service to a city 'expanding to greatness', as Auckland's mayor D. M. Robinson (1962) would have it. In the decade to 1961 the city's western sector had increased by over 165 per cent to rival central Auckland in population size. At the time, 17,000 acres were zoned for urban development in the west (Carr 1962: 45). Rutherford was there to shape that new population into productive, loyal citizens.

The school was a stone's throw away from the Northwestern Motorway, which, when completed in 1961, encouraged industry and shopping centres into the west, while also providing a direct route into the centre of Auckland. It was a corridor into the city for young New Zealanders who could legally drive from fifteen years of age, the youngest driving age in the developed world. The motorway was not a boon to all though. It dislodged business and required the removal of 15,000 inner-city homes, leading to the displacement of over 50,000 residents. Karangahape Road – 'K-road', Auckland's oldest street – became the site of a burgeoning strip club industry when the 'King of the g-string' Rainton Hastie moved in and established his Pink Pussy Cat Club in 1963.[1]

The Motorway, as a conceptual form, was captured in the work of Robert Ellis, one of New Zealand's most celebrated painters. In a preview of Ellis's 2014–15 exhibition in the Auckland Art Gallery, Peter Nunns (2014) said the artist 'showed the city in the process of expanding and mutating, and in the process creating a different New Zealand'. In this way, Ellis's work reflects the malleable city that, as Jonathan Raban (1988) put it, 'goes soft awaiting the imprint of an identity' (9). Later in 2015, a retrospective of 1960s new arts emanating from Auckland saw Ellis exhibited with street photographer Gary Baigent (1967) and filmmaker Rodney Charters, whose seminal *Film Exercise* (1966) featured the Northwestern Motorway – with a soundtrack from the La De Da's. For Kevin Borich, the motorway opened up the city's nightspots, providing access to musicians that played there: 'Max [Merritt] was my favourite and I used to go and get educated by driving forty miles into Auckland to watch these guys play' (*Australian Songwriter* 2014). Along with Merritt, the Auckland venues introduced him to Mick Leyton (Merseymen), jazzman Tommy Adderley, band leader Howard Morrison and Samoan/German pop of The Keil Isles, providing crucial experiences for the young guitarist's development (Reekie 2014).

In 1963, Borich and Brett Nielsen enrolled in Rutherford. By the end of that year the principal discerned students showed a 'new softness', a term first addressed to young, troubled American soldiers in Korea (Kinkead 1957). In an editorial in the school's Yearbook, the principal argued this condition would manifest itself in 'indulgent parents asking for pupils to be excused from Phys Ed., cross country runs, sport and [students] doing homework with the radio or television blaring' (*Rutherford Yearbook* 1963). While Rutherford was one of the first high schools to promote arts in its curriculum, in the early 1960s sport dominated as a measure of success. By the 1970s, Rutherford had gained a reputation for its disciplinarian approach. Brett Nielsen recalled that Borich, his classmate, was not allowed to join the school formal in 1963 because his tie was too narrow and his shoes were too pointy (Nielsen). The principal's dire warning was in light of Rutherford's decision that the 1964 senior students' class should set school standards. While Nielsen took his leave from school in December 1963 and began work in warehouses and on building sites, Borich continued studying in the 1964 school year as one of those senior students – but for Kevin the radio *was* his homework as he taped songs from the BBC World Service programmes to share with his bandmates (Borich). In the end, he and his

Rutherford friends took the soft option and disappeared into the city to become full-time musicians, earning a living of sorts playing covers in the late-night music scene. Soon, the broader social tensions that haunted the principal's editorial would play out with protests about New Zealand soldiers in Vietnam part of a cultural revolt that swept Auckland in the mid-1960s, culminating at the end of the decade in a series of bombings that rocked the city (Bollinger 2022; Edmonds 2021).

Auckland was becoming a city of shifting identities and social disparity where private was made public every day on the street. Working-class suburbs became streets for working girls and outer suburban rurality was being replaced by retailers. At the same time, mass formations began to shrink towards common interests. Public transport was privatized as the car and the motorcycle mobilized desires and dreams and encouraged smaller circles of sociality: the group, a gang, bands. The archetypal 'band' would ideally, equipment and all, fit into someone's car or a friend's van and would rehearse in an empty garage. Outside of that, small venues populated by regular fans were the mainstay of groups that had only just begun to conceive of constructing a public through media alone. The 1960s were also a time of stifling reaction against modernity and change. In New Zealand, the beginning of the decade ushered in twelve years of conservative National government until in 1972 when Labour Party leader Norman Kirk, dubbed 'Big Norm' in a song from pop band Ebony, was elected prime minster. The decade in between saw increased tensions as an underclass emerged in Auckland and other cities. In particular 'the confiscation' – where Māori lands were taken for colonial enterprise – continued to undermine indigenous well-being, breaking up familial networks and forcing many into decades of displacement. Rutherford played its part in this reaction. Donald Elley suggested that, by the 1970s, Rutherford was 'the most repressive government high school on the planet' (Elley 2017). These tensions come to be reflected in the music of the La De Da's as they moved from the suburban identity of The Mergers to the harder edged sound and fashion of garage bands found in urban communities from the 1960s and then later through mod and soul music. Their first hit 'How Is the Air Up There' reflected a keen sense of the social disparity evident in Auckland. Later self-penned songs – such as 'All-Purpose Low', a #3 hit on the New Zealand chart but banned in Australia – also showed a sharp observation of middle-class hypocrisy.[2] *The Happy Prince* album, which was written from early 1967 through to the end of 1968, would take this idea of social disparity and shape it into the band's first grand work and an early concept album, then a novel approach to pop-rock music anywhere in the world.

Migration underpinned Auckland's dynamism and that was exemplified in the La De Da's members' European, Scandinavian, Māori, and English backgrounds. Kevin Borich's family lived in Huapai at the far end of the Northwestern Motorway. His mother was born in Dalmatia (near Croatia) and immigrated to New Zealand with her family when she was five years old. Borich recalled his parents 'worked … seven days a week, to create a wonderful, highly productive orchard' in Huapai (Reekie op.cit.). Borich was committed to recording music before he had started at Rutherford. He recorded a song with his neighbours, Judy and Sue Donaldson. Soon after, the sisters became The Chicks and went on to become a popular television and club act (Caddick 2017).[3]

Borich's 1962/3 classmate Brett Nielsen was a keen drummer. His mother was an accomplished pianist, a musical autodidact who became a music teacher. His father carried on the Nielsen brass tradition and played sousaphone while his uncle played euphonium. Brett's Norwegian heritage – his grandfather had been one of the early settlers in Scandinavian enclave of Dannevirke at the bottom of the North Island – provided the family with an austere moral code that saw Brett's father stepping out with the Auckland Salvation Army band from the age of six. Later the elder Nielsen began playing with a Dixieland band, entertaining patrons on the city's racecourses. Brett was tapping out tunes with cutlery on the kitchen table until his parents secured a snare drum for him from his uncle. By this time, the family had moved from their inner-city abode to the new houses on the Te Atatù Peninsula, just a short bike ride away from Rutherford High (Nielsen).

When Borich was looking for some support for a performance his father had arranged at the local Huapai cricket club, Nielsen joined him with his snare playing Elvis's songs and standards. Soon after they added a bass guitarist, Trevor Wilson, to play 'the cricket dos' (Nielsen) and the three of them formed The Mergers, an instrumentals dance band. Wilson had joined Rutherford High School in 1963, a year below the other boys. He was from a single parent home in the inner western Auckland suburb of Westmere, where his mother, who had migrated from England, ran the local fish and chip shop. It was through Wilson that The Mergers gained their fourth member, Māori singer and guitarist Phil Key. When Key joined the group late in 1963, he was taking guitar lessons from jazz player Johnny Bradfield and living in Point Chevalier, an adjacent suburb to Westmere, with his family including an older brother Dennis, and sister Adrienne. Point Chev, as the area was known, had been the site of a large public housing development in the 1930s. The Keys were one of the few Maori families living in the area (Dennis Key). After the Second World War, as rural Huapai was joined to the urban centre by Auckland's motorways, the inner-city beach suburbs of Westmere and Point Chevalier were turned into backwaters. In the immediate post-war years, trams brought plenty of Auckland's citizens to the harbour beaches. Once the Auckland Harbour Bridge was open in 1959, increased car ownership saw the inner harbour city beach become less popular and businesses that had thrived on the summer trade were relocated. The tramlines were removed during the 1950s, but the broad thoroughfare of Point Chevalier Road was a reminder of the era before cars changed the city. The area maintained a vibrant local population with educational aspirations fed by the nearby Grammar school in Mount Albert, which Phil Key attended. Later, after the band began playing as the La De Da's at the Platterack, another fellow of British background stepped up to be the fifth member of the group. Bruce Howard's maternal grandmother was born in Arrochar Scotland and later immigrated from Hellensburgh on the Clyde to New Zealand (Melanie and Denis Winters, personal communication). In New Zealand, at the time The Mergers were playing, guitar bands were hugely popular; however, The Beatles phenomenon was already on the horizon.

Brett Nielsen recalled when his group first encountered The Beatles. It was all tied up with girls and youthful intimations of sex. It was late in 1963, and the boys were all around fifteen years old. Kevin Borich, who was the musical leader at this stage and would remain the social glue for the band, had a car and he took the other Rutherford boys to a small party set up by his girlfriend in a shed at the back of her parent's place. She brought her friends and a portable record player. Into this mix of 'spin-the-bottle', secret kiss-and-don't-tell, music and intimacy came a hot new release: The Beatles' 'I Want to Hold Your Hand'. 'Hearing that for the first time, the strength of singing and playing, we'd never heard anything like it. You know the other stuff we were listening to was pretty much standards. But this … what the hell was this?' (Nielsen). It is easy now, at a distance of some decades, to overlook the innovation of pop songs such as 'I Want to Hold Your Hand'. It was, as Ian Macdonald (1995) has declared, 'a revolution in the head'. The song was explicitly written for the US market where Capitol at the time were still not issuing Beatles singles. Macdonald describes it as 'blatant contrivance … It was exciting, unexpected, irreverent … "I Want to Hold Your Hand" electrified American pop … aspiring American players and writers listened to The Beatles' free-spirited unorthodoxies in excited disbelief' (76, 77). And so did The Mergers. The song provided the first US hit single for The Beatles and was quickly followed by 'Please Please Me', which had been a massive hit in the UK months earlier. With these chart-topping songs out, The Beatles toured the United States in early 1964 and followed that with a tour to New Zealand and Australia in June that year. The following year however the Liverpudlians' wit and sophistication were thrown into relief by the 1965 tour of The Pretty Things, who demonstrated just how wild music and musicians could be. Rodney Charters recalled seeing the band in New Plymouth: 'They were pretty wild as musicians. [They] just had a driving sound that nobody in New Zealand had ever heard before, up in your face' (Charters). The Beatles were just one aspect of the broad social revolution represented by beat music.

If Borich's connection with savvy young women prompted The Mergers to reconsider their act, a more constant connection with Phil Key's sister, Adrienne, cemented their musical knowledge. An avid music collector, she introduced them to records from lesser-known British and hard-line American R&B groups, providing the band with the bulk of their early repertoire (Dennis Key; Sergent; Gillanders & Welsh 2019: 159). Initially, Key's voice was not appreciated within the group but slowly, as singing and harmonizing became crucial for a band to be booked to play covers at local dances, Key became the focus, taking on lead vocals. Once Key was ensconced as the singer, The Mergers re-emerged as the La De Da's.[4]

For all the impression that the early Beatles made on the band members, it was not the music that they began to make. Ironically, the only Lennon-McCartney song they recorded – 'Come Together' (1969) – was their last recording as the largely original line-up (Nielsen had left the band late in 1967). The introduction to a harder blues sound through Adrienne Key's music collection was complemented by off-air cassette tapes from Kevin Borich's 'homework': recording the BBC's 'Top of the Pops' programme that was re-broadcast on New Zealand's ZB stations from 1964. The ZB stations, a state-owned public broadcasting network, were generally not inclined to play pop and rock music. New Zealand record companies were also very conservative with new releases and sometimes it was months before an international chart song found its way to New Zealand stores.[5] The inordinate delay for new releases and a lack of commercial advertising were some of the issues that prompted the formation of Auckland's offshore pirate broadcasters, Radio Hauraki, in December 1966. Meanwhile, Borich's standing in the group was enhanced by introducing new material to the band: 'You could tape songs on Thursday, rehearse them on Friday and be playing them live on Saturday night three months or so before they were released locally' (Gillanders and Welsh: 159). Borich's skill with guitar meant the La De Da's tended to a rockier sound immediately. When

Bruce Howard joined with his Ekosonic organ – an inexpensive, lightweight, transistorized keyboard that emulated other instruments – the band's sound became unique in Auckland. Howard, like Trevor Wilson, had an English migrant background and his incorporation into the band began to shift the weight of musical influence. Living on the city's north shore he was the only one not from the west. Howard had trained as a musician, and he brought a lyrical and musical sophistication that would eventually displace Borich's influence and lead the band on the journey to record *The Happy Prince*.

I suggested earlier that accident and coincidence shaped the La De Da's formation. Change and openness to chance were always important in their becoming musicians. The band was both willing to experiment musically and open to adapting their identity. They soaked up influences as a sugar cube soaked up acid. Their first chance to record came in 1965 due to a deal they did with a promoter to perform a lip-sync cover of the theme from a film, *Those Magnificent Men in Their Flying Machines*, on television. The song was not at all relevant to their repertoire; it even threatened the image they wished to project as they had to dress up in nineteenth-century clobber. But this was less important than the opportunity it presented. For payment they were provided with studio time to record a single. They recorded two of their own songs rather than the cover versions of popular tunes that they churned out in Auckland dances and nightspots. While the deal only provided for a small pressing, which was released in April 1965 and distributed by the band, the record, particularly the 'B' side 'Little Girl' (written by Kevin Borich and Trevor Wilson), has become a garage classic. While the A side 'Ever since that night' (Borich) is something of an embarrassment now ('that terrible song' as Borich described it), the record was an indication that the band aimed to chart their own course. It was also a measure of their distance, at that time, from an industry that often insisted on covers of songs that the local studio had a license on. The band also took every opportunity to get out in front of an audience, and their enthusiasm and great sound led to a recommendation from respected Auckland guitarist, Red McKelvie, that they try out for a fill-in residency at the Platterack, a two-floor, dingy venue close to the CBD. They got the gig and impressed the management so much they were given the permanent residency. By December 1965, when most of the members were still only seventeen years old, they were fully professional, earning their living from gigs.

The Auckland scene

In early 1960s' Auckland, you may have found Buckminster Fuller arguing that he was once a long-lost Maori navigator (Tomkins 1965) or seen Irish theatrical innovator Micheál MacLiammóir's lone hand performance as Oscar Wilde. You may have caught a long-haired Barry Humphries in a teen venue dancing, 'jerky, almost spastic, yet perfectly rhythmical [with] [t]he crowd pressed around him, cheering him on' (Stead 1992: 326), or seen concerts by Ravi Shankar or Thelonious Monk. These fleeting moments of cultural intensity demonstrate the city's diversity and opportunity. As we have seen for Kevin Borich, the Auckland scene provided for the La De Da's education. They were recognized as musicians and in their newly professional personae they regularly caught up with such musicians as jazz pianist Claude Papesch (who would produce their 1967 hit single, 'Hey Baby') and guitarist Doug Jerebine (Neilsen). They mixed with the boho crowd from Auckland University's Elam

School of Art, where Robert Ellis taught and innovators like future Hollywood television director, Rodney Charters were students.

The University was at the edge of the inner city and the student crowd was a large element of Auckland's night-time entertainment. In the daytime, though, the city was the domain of the young urban worker: clerks, shop assistants, typists. The 'soft city' drew in people to develop an identity, to adopt a modern style and become someone new. The late 1950s saw the emergence of a 'teenage' audience in Auckland, as in many other post-war cities around the world. This novel audience, made up of age groups from thirteen to twenty-five, had become possible due to the electrification and amplification of music – and with the ready work available to young people who could leave school at age fifteen in New Zealand. These conditions, along with broadcasting, allowed for a music industry where goods, services and identities could be manufactured and traded. As Colin MacInnes put it, it was a business of 'absolute beginners' (1959). There were killings to be made from the right combination of music and performance, distribution and exploitation. In his survey of the Auckland, scene from 1955 to 1970, Roger Watkins (1995) mapped thirty band venues in Auckland's CBD. From the Beatle Inn and the Shiralee, just off Quay Street near the ferry terminals, through The Top Twenty and Platterack tucked away in the lanes between Wyndham and Victoria, all the way up to the Hi Diddle Griddle and St Seps high on the Khyber Pass above The Domain, Auckland's venues and nightspots were pumping with live music. With the motorways as much as the docks feeding in punters there was a heady mix of international and local cultures attending to what the venues offered. Changing fashions, emerging cultural trends, new professions – all opened up opportunities for young people making their way in the city.

Hugh Lynn and Robyn (Bobi) Nicholas became important to the La De Da's story as they made new careers for themselves in Auckland. Both born in 1943 they were at least five years older than the band members. Lynn made a name and a living servicing the day time dreams and night time industries of the Auckland scene. From a thespian family, Lynn was a dancer from thirteen years old, gaining experience in Auckland's rock and roll competitions. Later, while still at school, he became a ballet dancer but was bullied by schoolmates so he took up martial arts. Lynn was just as good at that as he was at dancing. Venues wanted trained bouncers and Lynn founded a security firm to fill that need. He became a compere for Top Twenty, which, like other venues, needed go-go dancers. So, he set up an evening school at his mother's dance studio in downtown Auckland, training young women as dancers for the city venues (Lynn). This background set him up to be the road manager of choice when the band did their first national tour in 1967. Robyn Nicholas (later Petch) was fifteen in 1958 when she began working as a shorthand/typist in a city trading company – the precursor to department stores – and attending lunch time gigs in central Auckland. Five years later she was style maker and friend to emerging stars and within a decade she became a crucial link in the La De Da's career as a booking manager for the Sydney based Cordon Bleu agency.

Fashion, music, media

Robyn, her parents and older sister Denise, a dressmaker and model, lived in Devonport on Auckland's North Shore, just down from North Head Army Camp. Devonport is at the end of the peninsula that formed the northern side of the Waitematā Harbour. Commuting meant catching the ferry across the harbour to the city centre, until the Harbour Bridge opened in 1959. Working in Auckland's old commercial institutions gave Robyn portable skills that encouraged her to travel. Her older sister had already moved to Sydney, and in September 1962, Robyn took the passenger liner, the SS *Orsova*, across the Tasman to Australia. For a year she worked for an insurance agency, changing her name to Bobi because there were too many other 'Robyns' working in the agency. She was also introduced to the new fashions and mod styles arriving in Australia from England (Petch).

On her return to Auckland in 1963, the renamed Bobi Nicholas brought the new fashion sense with her and found she was in vogue with the changes occurring in her home city. Now twenty years old, Nicholas began modelling. Street fashion had become an important component of music and popular culture. Whether through stage performances or broadcasting, street fashions – clothes and hair styles – were a crucial link between audiences and their new music idols. In the small lanes behind Auckland's larger thoroughfares, venues were joined by hairdressers and clothes boutiques catering to young men and women who worked and played in the city. In the late southern hemisphere summer of 1963, Nicholas was booked for lunchtime coffee shop parades by The Casual Shop, a new venture from young fashion entrepreneur Diana Dent (Graham Dent, her husband, later became a key link in popular music between New Zealand and Australia, as I discuss in the next chapter). At The Casual Shop, Nicholas met Jackie Holme and together they frequented The Shiralee and the Top Twenty that featured bands like Max Merritt and the Meteors. Soon

Jackie was going out with Max, who travelled over the Bridge to Devonport in his 1950s XK150 Jaguar to take the women for picnics around the harbour and to the hot springs west of Auckland (Petch).

As well as selling mod clothes from Quant and other British boutiques, The Casual Shop sold their own contemporary fashion items. Jackie Holme had begun cutting hair for Dent's amateur models in the back room at The Casual Shop and was soon very good at copying Vidal Sassoon's classic bob cut, a natural choice for Bobi. Before long Jackie's talents were legendary – she conducted her hairdressing with fabric shears. When singer Diane Jacobs was in town looking for a new image, she found Jackie, who styled her with a Vidal Sassoon bob as well. Jacobs also met Nicholas at The Casual Shop; they became friends and soon the singer had also changed her name – to Dinah Lee. She explained how fashion, style and the city provided the opportunity for a new identity:

> I used to have a bouffant haircut – the rocker image – and she [Jackie] just got me and cut my hair in the back of a boutique that used to be there. She cut my hair and put on all these clothes, and away I went. The whole image completely changed. Gone was the Diane Jacobs image – Dinah Lee appeared. As soon as I got this new image it was a completely new character that sort of took me over all of a sudden. It was like, 'Yes, this is good … I like this … this is *me*.'
>
> (Bourke 2013)

For many, Dinah Lee epitomized the link between youth, fashion and music in 1960s New Zealand. In 2021 Doris de Pont, the founder of the New Zealand Fashion Museum, reflected on these links noting that: 'Pop stars like Dinah Lee … helped disseminate the new look' (2021). In 1964, not yet twenty-one, Dinah Lee released her debut single. The following year, when Lee moved to Australia, Bobi Nicholas was already there, having once again taken on Sydney as a home with her friend Jackie Holme, who was dating Australian rocker Billy Thorpe. Nicholas, meanwhile, had found contract work as a department store model with Farmers department store in Sydney. When that stint ended after six months she refused a store job, and fortune took a hand. When Nicholas learned that Diana Dent would open The Casual Shop in Sydney, she became their first store manager. The Casual Shop's Sydney presence from June 1965 was just one part of a larger cultural invasion of Australia by New Zealanders that had begun after Ray Columbus and The Invaders scored a hit in the Sydney charts in 1964 with 'She's a Mod' and followed it up with live television appearances and a series of performances at the iconic Surf City in Kings Cross. When Dinah Lee arrived in Sydney in September 1965 to begin a year-long series of engagements around Australia, her manager Jim Haddleton asked Nicholas to be her personal assistant. She also became her flatmate. This began Bobi Nicholas's career in music. Three years later, in 1968, after her Australian engagements, Dinah Lee travelled to the United States and England, but Bobi stayed in Sydney. Bobi went on to have an important role in the La De Da's' permanent shift to Sydney in 1968, by which time she was running the booking agency Cordon Bleu for entrepreneur Harry Widmer. Cordon Bleu had signed up the La De Da's for their Sydney residencies.

Early in 1966, the La De Da's residency at the Platterack established them in Auckland as a band with a hard musical edge and a dress style all their own. From here the band began their conquest of the New Zealand charts. By the end of the year, they had released their eponymous debut album.

Between January 1966 and August 1967, the band had five New Zealand top ten hits: 'How Is the Air Up There?', 'On Top of the World', 'Hey Baby', 'All Purpose Low' and 'Rosalie'. Musician Peter Grattan recalled the impact of the La De Da's on him:

> [O]ur Whangarei band [Whangarei is a city north of Auckland] was in awe of them, had tartan trousers just like their's [sic]! We played support and backed Maria Dallas for the Loxene Gold Disc Show […] with the 'La des' watching offstage. We were in awe of Bruce's Ekosonic organ, and Brett Nielsen had the biggest ride cymbal I've ever seen, I hit it and it hurt my wrist! But what a buzz getting to play his red onyx Rogers kit.
>
> (Grattan)

Trevor's bass on a later La De Da's hit, 'On top of the world', inspired a young Mike Chunn (Split Enz) to take up bass (Gillanders & Welsh: 162). Christine Mintrom was new to the city arriving from the provinces in 1966, when she heard the band at the Platterack: 'Their singer has an amazing voice. The organ intrigues me and gives the band a sound I haven't been aware of at other dances in Auckland since I've been there … They are wearing street clothes, not suits like all the other Auckland bands' (Mintrom 2018). The band certainly took time with their look. The origins of the tartan trousers are not known, although it was generally believed to be the work of one of their mothers. Phil added modern street dress, skivvies and duffle coats. Brett's style was different again. His mother had set him up with an account at Vance Vivian, the famous New Zealand menswear store where he bought the sport coats that became his signature (Nielsen) (See Figure 1.1, the cover *Teen Beat*, October 1966).

The band was able to make the most of the emerging connection between fashion, music and television. November

1965 saw the inaugural national Golden Disc Award, sponsored by cosmetic company Loxene (won that year by Ray Columbus and the Invaders). In 1966, the La De Da's debut professional recording, 'How Is the Air Up There?' made it to the final list of songs in contention for the Award. While they did not win,

Figure 1.1 *Cover band. The fashion conscious band was featured in* Teen Beat *on the occasion of their debut album,* La De Da's *(1966), which consisted entirely of covers.* The Happy Prince *(1969) was the band's first album of original songs.*

that band received exposure through their live performance broadcast with other finalists, in a one-hour television special. These early broadcasts came out of Wellington, home of the international HMV label, but by the beginning of 1967, the centre of music television had moved to Auckland. The New Zealand Broadcasting Corporation (NZBC) began screening a new weekly pop music programme, *C'mon*, from their Shortland Street studios. By now Kevin Borich's former neighbours, the Donaldson sisters, were fully fledged pop stars who performed as The Chicks on *C'mon*. They sang and danced and dressed in brightly coloured mini-skirts by designer Annie Bonza, who had recently returned to Auckland after living a bohemian life in Sydney married to artist Mike Brown. *C'mon* gave Bonza the opportunity to put her experimental clothing designs to a larger audience. The La De Da's 1966 Golden Disc performance set them up as an exciting television act and they were often featured on *C'mon* during its three-year run.

While television was increasingly the vehicle for national promotion, radio remained largely localized with the NZBC stations based in the major cities: Auckland and Wellington on the North Island, and Christchurch and Dunedin on the South. Even the pirate broadcasters that began operating in international waters of Hauraki Gulf north of Auckland in December 1966 largely only broadcast to an Auckland audience. Consequently, radio played a role in establishing artists as a product of local influences and helped maintained local scenes in each of the cities. As a teenager in Christchurch, Rodney Coe was immersed in the local music scene. He played in bands and worked as a technician at the local NZBC station when he left school in 1961. He and his friends always took particular interest in the Auckland bands and made time to see them when they toured: 'They always seemed to be a step ahead as to what the trends were in terms of what they played and how they worked. So, they were always an inspiration to us' (Coe). He recalled hearing the La De Da's 'How Is the Air Up There?' on the Christchurch station: '[I thought] wow, that's fantastic! What a great rock band. They really stood out as being something special at the time.' Nearly a decade later, as an EMI technician in Sydney, Coe worked with the renewed La De Da's line-up to produce *Rock and Roll Sandwich* in 1973, the first album for the band after *The Happy Prince* was released in 1969.

Production and innovation: The Auckland recordings

While Wellington hosted production facilities for HMV, the multinational label that later merged with EMI, Auckland was home to a group of innovative independent studios with dedicated producers 'that helped revolutionise the recording process' in New Zealand (Grigg 2018). Studios like Astor, Viking and James Productions had great catalogues, but it is generally agreed that Eldred Stebbing's Studios and the Zodiac label had the most influence on Auckland and New Zealand's music in the 1960s. Most notably it was the vehicle for the Australian success of 'She's A Mod' for Ray Columbus and the Invaders. The La De Da's 1966 single 'How Is the Air Up There?' established their relationship with Stebbing's Studios, where they proceeded to record all their Auckland material. Later that year they also signed up as the house band at Galaxie, the venue Stebbing owned.

Eldred Stebbing, the patriarch of the Stebbing family business, was always on the look-out for a new, profitable band to produce. When he became aware of the buzz around the

La De Da's, Eldred 'and another "suit"', as Borich recalls, came to their show at the Platterack (Gillanders and Welsh: 160) with a copy of a recording by US duo, The Changin' Times. The La De Da's rehearsed the song and then played it for Stebbing and producer John Hawkins who agreed to record them. The recording session was memorable for Borich as it afforded him the first opportunity to record with a fuzz box which Eldred's son, Robert, had made up in his workshop. It was, he believed, 'probably the first time a fuzz box had been used in a New Zealand recording' (Borich). Robert Stebbing's penchant for technical innovation was one of the reasons why the Stebbing studio was an important part of the Auckland music story.[6] Stebbing had licencing arrangements with the international Philips label whose representative John McCready had brought 'How Is the Air Up There?' to Stebbing. In 1966, Philips was expanding its roster of artists on its own label as it managed changing industry circumstances. For whatever reason, Stebbing released the La De Da's single on Philips rather than Zodiac. The track itself was a great fit for the band with its astringent lyrics that hint at psychedelic influences that would come later: 'When you get tired / Of your lonely life in high society / Well, get some kicks and take a trip / And come on down with me'. That seam of social hypocrisy was also mined in their first completely self-penned album, *The Happy Prince*, and there is just enough ambiguity in the 'take a trip' line – maybe they were referring to the Motorway – to justify Nielsen's observation that chemical drugs were virtually non-existent in New Zealand and that it was only later in Melbourne that acid came to influence the band (Nielsen; Gillanders and Welsh: 162). The song allowed Howard's organ to come to the fore with swirling trills. Add in the distorted guitar and a thumping bass and you have a classic garage band rocker. Historically, the song claims the distinction of being the first local track to make it into the newly minted National Hit Parade – it rose to #4.

Following the success of 'How Is the Air Up There?' the band, in typical fashion, put to Stebbing that they wanted to record their own material. The studio was committed to licence arrangements and initially resisted the band's suggestion but finally agreed to record a Howard/Wilson composition 'Don't You Stand in My Way' backed with a cover of 'I Get What I Want', which was written in part by Isaac Hayes. The songs ironically referenced the La De Da's ethos of autonomy, a quality that would also bedevil their commercial success. The record's sound shifted towards the soul music that the band was experimenting with in its club covers. The song did not get a run on the local charts but 'Don't You Stand in My Way' has achieved a certain immortality as part of the soundtrack to *Film Exercise*, the first ever film that emerged from Auckland's Elam School. Still Stebbing's studio remained suspicious of the band charting their own direction, even as they encouraged their idiosyncratic interpretation of already licenced songs. When the band released a cover of 'Hey Baby' in 1967, it became their first number one hit. They were apparently taken to heart by the local gay community, possibly due to the campy telephone answering effect dropped in towards the end of the song. Another self-penned composition later in 1967, 'All-Purpose Low' (Wilson/Howard), provided an indication that theatrical interpretations were filtering into the band's songwriting. By this time, they were already thinking of songs structured around the 'Happy Prince' story. 'All-Purpose Low' was not penned to become part of that album which was finally recorded in Sydney in 1969, but the song demonstrated the influence of inventive song-making by contemporary British bands like the Kinks and The Who. From an initial shouted call to attention, the band shifts into a fairground-style melody with lyrics highlighting social hypocrisy. As the track develops, it shifts register again, into a rollicking crescendo only to drop once more into the fairground tune, followed by one more chorus and an abrupt end. As a pop song it is baffling, but it made it to No.3 on the Hit Parade chart and contributed to the growing mystique around the band.

Conclusion

The band had a year of incredible success from when they went professional in late 1965. 1966 became their breakout year capped by a top-selling debut album of covers released late in December. In January 1967, they embarked on their first national tour of New Zealand and May that year saw their initial Australian foray. This visit was well timed. It coincided with the release of their ground-breaking second album that began to showcase the group's original compositions and the band had their first No. 1 hit in New Zealand, 'Hey Baby!'. Sydney and Melbourne, however, threw up challenges and opportunities that changed the band. Musically they continued to expand and experiment with their repertoire and the band's autonomy remained important as they continued to chart their own course without a manager. Although they had a road manager for their national tour, the band had all but taken control of their own music. This was not the kind of band that Stebbing Studios needed. Eldred believed they had grown too big. He told Gillanders and Welsh:

> The trouble is you get personality problems coming into it. Once these guys think they are 'on top of the world', excuse

the pun (ed: 'On Top Of The World' was a La De Da's hit song) they start trying to dictate what they want to do and that's where the problems start: if you're going to devote your whole life to them, yeah that's alright but you're never going to make any money out of it. (169)

While Stebbing was ostensibly setting up a deal for the band to record songs for their third album, *The Happy Prince*, with Ivan Dayman's Sunshine Records label in Sydney, the studio was effectively walking away from the band. In the end the Sydney session for Sunshine was a disaster, setting the band's recording schedule back for months. The album was eventually picked up by EMI but not before another major setback with an independent label. It took private funding from Widmer, owner of the Cordon Bleu booking agency, as well as energy from the enigmatic poet, Adrian Rawlins, who had built a strong belief in the band's project, to finally record the album. The development of this complex arrangement is the subject of the final chapter, but for now it is important to explore the allure and cultural cachet of Oscar Wilde and 'The Happy Prince' as the band worked to establish themselves as a credible, artistic ensemble.

2 'Don't You Stand in My Way'

Introduction

The La De Da's self-penned single, 'Don't You Stand in My Way', while not a chart success, was a critical point in the band's career. The band fought their producers to get the song recorded, probably clinching their estrangement from Stebbing. The studio sessions were also used to record the soundtrack for New Zealand's earliest student film, *Film Exercise* (Charters 1966). This experimental film, born of the Auckland scene, reflected the tensions that were becoming evident for those immersed in the inner-city milieu. 'Don't You Stand in My Way' was integral to the narrative. Music historians Marks and McIntyre (2010) argue 'Don't You Stand in My Way' is a marker of the band's development: 'Driven by a buzz-saw riff, righteous handclaps, Ray Charles inspired keyboard work, and Phil Key's rich throaty vocals, 'Don't You Stand in My Way' demonstrates why the La De Da's were New Zealand's top R&B/soul combo' (181). Unlike their previous single with Stebbing, the song was not a hit, but the dedication of the band to record their own material was critical. It took until *The Happy Prince* for the band to produce an album wholly of their own songs. In this chapter, we explore the cultural well-springs of that creative endeavour.

Soundtrack

Film Exercise was exactly that – an exercise: a student's audio-visual essay 'with sequences in different styles', edited to the band's soundtrack (*Unseen City* 2015).[1] The ten-minute wordless film was produced, shot and edited by second year Elam Arts student, Rodney Charters. It was done with little money, Charters paying for the film himself: 'The School in Auckland had no equipment at all … to acquire the equipment [I had to] beg and borrow around town' (Charters). With his father's 16mm Bolex, a car borrowed from advertising executive Bob Harvey, and editing time cadged from downtime in an Auckland television studio, Charters pieced together a film that became a signifier of 1960s Auckland. Once he had the footage, prior to editing, Charters began to think of the soundtrack. This footage had no dialogue so the soundtrack would be crucial to carry the film's narrative. As luck would have it Charters approached the La De Da's at an opportune time: 'I had decided that they were the hottest thing in town and I went to where they were doing a club gig … They loved the idea [of doing a soundtrack]. They were laying tracks [at Stebbing's Studios] so the timing was perfect' (See Figure 2.1. Kevin Borich at the sessions). Charters attended studio sessions for the recording and worked with the band on some sections:

> [T]here was a particular rhythm that I wanted, that I had heard on a track an English short film, about railway, steam trains during the winter [likely *Snow* (1963)]. [It] had this lovely drum riff … They said, 'Oh, that's a paradiddle'. So, we did a paradiddle drum track … and that was part of the pulsing of the motorcycle, winding through those hills.

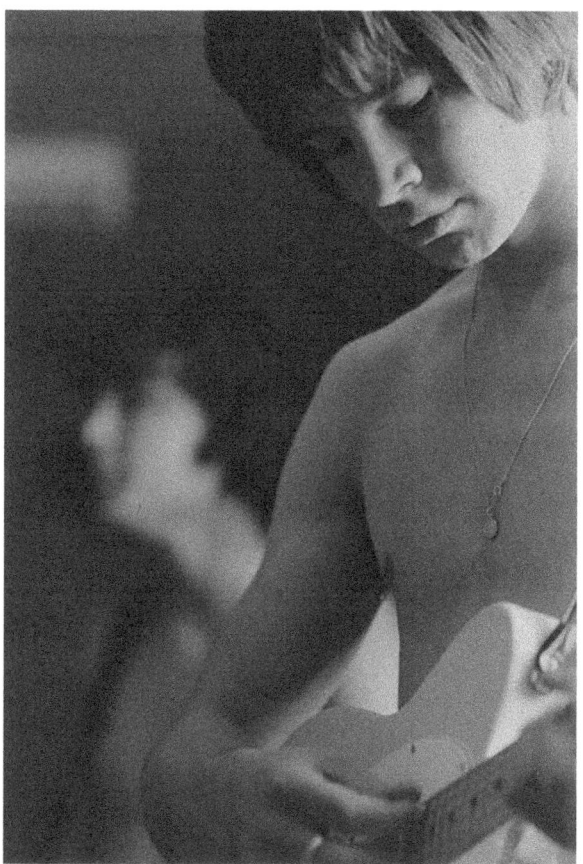

Figure 2.1 *Kevin Borich at the sessions for 'Don't You Stand in My Way'. Rodney Charters Collection.*

Creating a soundtrack fed into the band's enthusiasm for novelty and experimentation and provided an opportunity to expand the band's writing and performance.

For a first-time student film, *Film Exercise* achieved considerable success. It was screened in the 1968 Sydney and Melbourne Film Festivals, winning its category at Sydney. The film helped Charters enter Royal College of Film in London and he is now a successful film and television cinematographer in Hollywood. *Film Exercise* featured Charters' fellow arts student Ted Spring and Shelly Gane, an architecture undergraduate who had worked as Charters's subject for a portfolio of fashion portrait photographs (Gane, personal communication). From the film's establishing shot on West Auckland's remote beaches, we find a wild-haired, barefoot muse (Gane) who attaches herself to a bike and biker (Spring). When muse meets motorbike the La De Da's soundtrack begins and soon becomes a mournful, melodic vocal chant. While echoing Ennio Morricone's theme from *The Good, the Bad and the Ugly* (1966), the band lifted the chant from The Yardbirds' 'Still I'm Sad' (it was reworked again for the title track of the album *Find Us A Way* (May 1967)).[2] Covers for the La De Da's were more than just fillers for band routines: they provided opportunities for the band to quote their musical influences. Interpretation was a legitimate creative form and, later, bands such as Vanilla Fudge, with their own takes on contemporary popular songs, were inspirational as the band developed their musical performances.

With the muse riding pillion – literally a second skin – the biker speeds across the remote, desolate beach, traversing tree-lined coastal roads to arrive in the city at night as the soundtrack shifts to a soulful blues: the band's take on Booker T and the MG's 'Green Onions'. Howard's Ekosonic organ's melodic line is punctuated by Borich's guitar stabs while Wilson and Nielsen provide a steady beat. Lights and pedestrians give way finally to a party scene in a suburban house. Here the biker enters and is greeted by back-slapping buddies and, with beer bottle in hand, he disappears into a darkened party room. The muse/bike remains outside in the semi-dark, apart from an ominous 'reflection' shot where Gane appears in a mirror in the entrance hall. At this point the La De Da's single 'Don't You Stand in My Way' takes hold of the narrative.

The film itself marks a redefinition of nature within an urban milieu. In this audio-visual essay, the motorbike links the wild freedom of Auckland's west coast to the dark anonymity of the city. The muse is both freedom and threat. The wildness of nature that inheres to the biker is abandoned at the point where the companiable culture of 'the scene' takes over. While beer was the drug depicted in the film, increasingly chemicals and 'weed' (marijuana) were being used recreationally. LSD (lysergic acid diethylamide) was legal in New Zealand until late 1967 and 'pills' (generally prescription amphetamines) were common in Auckland venues. Drugs – legal or illegal – were a way to experiment with a loss of control and the subsequent experience of 'being free'. The film depicts tensions in how this freedom could be experienced: between Arcadian idyll and urban excitement; muse and mates; women and men. 'Don't You Stand in My Way' is a masculine injunction against the limits of these relationships within a youthful milieu where everything seemed attainable for some. The song calls out those who would stand in the way of sensual experience: 'I'm breaking out don't stand in my way / If you do, you'll have a nervous day / I'm sick of people preaching to me / I'm breaking out, don't try to hold me'. Within this perspective, beauty, nature, femininity and authority combine to provide a moral brake on experience which can be overcome by men abandoning innocence.[3] Why not try to have it all? Why grow up, when youth validated both excess and responsibility – even if this was simply a responsibility to experience? In the film – and by extension the La De Da's track – 'nature', while a source of inspiration, was not necessarily to be trusted when the aim was to have fun.[4] In *Film Exercise* nature is represented as contested freedom, where dangerous worldly innocence (the muse at the door) is trumped by internalised experience (the darkened party room). The landscape that would be explored most fervently in similar 'scenes' around the globe during the 1960s was not an Arcadian rural idyll, but an inner landscape, where drugs were crucial to accessing an altered state of mind with which one could perceive the world anew.

Psychedelia: Alternatives and interpretations

For some the relationship between drugs and music shaped the counterculture of the 1960s (Riley 2019; Selvin 1995; Stephens 1998). As George Case (2010) noted, scientists, scholars and literary celebrities were among those who claimed: 'Mind altering drugs … were the means by which a sexually-repressed, death-obsessed Western culture could finally redeem itself into something peaceful, life affirming and cooperative' (44). Adding a layer of critique to the contemporary analysis of 'psychedelic pop', Richard Middleton (1972) argued 'way-out' music was a reaction 'connected with the irrationality, the inhumanity, the "witches brew", which is our civilisation' (236–7). Either way, the countercultural critique that mainstream values were poison for which the antidote was 'freeing the mind' led to psychedelics – as both substances and style – being taken up broadly in 1960s society. Romantic notions of psychotropic drugs were prominent in popular music of the time. The relationship between Western values, music and the attainment of universal values was succinctly summed up by changing attitudes to Indian music and cultures. After moving permanently to Australia around 1968 Kevin Borich took up sitar, learning from a book he picked up on his initial visit to Sydney in 1967:

> I bought a book called *My Music My Life* by Ravi Shankar, which actually tells you how to tune the thing. And when I was in Australia, I bought one [a sitar]. It was such an amazing thing when you when you tune it. […] They play certain ragas, different scales. So they retune the sympathetic strings to resonate after each other. When you pick that note, and it's in tune, it will give that beautiful echo, that note will come alive and make the whole note last longer. So it's an amazing concept of the transference of energy. The cosmos!

Somewhere on Australia's east coast in the middle of 1968, the La De Da's became known as pop's 'psychedelic gods' (*Milesago*, 'Groups and solo artists: La De Das').

Despite the impact of psychedelic music, pop is not usually synonymous with the cultural underground. In his description of New Zealand's counterculture, Nick Bollinger (2022) rates the La De Da's only one mention, when the post *Happy Prince* version of the band – 'a stripped-down power trio' (210) – returned to Aotearoa in 1973 to play the Great Ngaruawahia Festival. Bollinger makes the point plainly: 'Bohemians didn't listen to pop music. Or if they did, they didn't take it seriously' (38). Still, with the credentials of their early penmanship it is worth considering how the counterculture may have impacted the La De Da's. Their initial single, 'How Is the Air Up There', captured disenchantment with mainstream values, and their earliest self-penned songs – 'Don't You Stand in My Way' and 'All-Purpose Low' – represented statements of social resistance. However, the cultural gap was real: the La De Da's were not considered as part of the countercultural revolt against values. It was in 1970s Wellington that underground bands like Blerta and Mammal were formed to play psychedelia, the popular music of the underground.

While there were attempts to create a psychedelic experience without drugs – famously by Sydney jazz musicians incorporating light shows into performances – engaging with the counterculture usually involved some pre-existing understanding of, as Hendrix would have it, 'being experienced'. In 1960s, New Zealand pop, though, drug culture was still largely frowned upon. Brett Nielsen has made the point that the band had never touched drugs – particularly psychedelics – until they went to Sydney and Melbourne later in 1967. Even Hugh Lynn, their road manager on the initial national tour, insisted there were no drugs involved. They were simply hard-working, dedicated musicians: professional entertainers with ambitions. Thus, the national tour they undertook in early 1967 was a part of a larger plan – to bankroll their aspirations to get to Sydney and eventually London. For that, a recording project was important. The tour provided a chance to talk out a project that suited these ambitions. Could a literary structure such as a fairy tale allow for a collection of songs with a strong artistic and social focus? Could this be a suitable project to take to the world?

From the Mergers and into the early La De Da's, Trevor Wilson and Kevin Borich had been the primary songwriters. Bruce Howard's musical skills changed the dynamic of the band providing opportunities to write more complex original songs. Brett Nielsen recalled: 'My impression was that the person in the band who had the musicality was Bruce Howard … Kevin was a good player, and he turned into a great player. But, at the early stages, most of the musical ideas, chord changes and all that sort of stuff, they would come from Bruce. He had that knowledge' (Nielsen). Borich's approach was to 'get lost in the sound': 'I wasn't into reading [music]. I was too busy with the guitar in my hand and trying to learn the chords. I didn't like getting taught music' (Borich). When Howard joined the band, he began to write music to which Trevor Wilson provided words. It was this combination that progressed the songwriting for *The Happy Prince*.

The La De Da's albums demonstrated a steady growth of writing original material through 1966 and into 1967. Their debut self-titled album, released late in 1966, consisted entirely of covers. On the next album (*Find Us a Way*, May 1967) half the songs were Bruce Howard and Trevor Wilson originals. 'Don't You Stand in My Way', their first song released as a single, stands out because its emotional tension comes from an attitude other than 'love', typically evident in commercial pop. As Bollinger notes, around this time '[t]he term "pop" was beginning to be supplanted by the weightier "rock"' (88) and 'Don't You Stand in My Way' is a candidate for an early local 'rock' song. Self-penned songs like 'Don't You Stand in My Way' and 'All-Purpose Low' demonstrated character-driven storytelling through songwriting that was developed further in *The Happy Prince*, the first complete album of their own songs. However, as mentioned earlier, covers were not simply to provide their chart success or fill in a live routine. First, their live audiences may not have heard the original version which was unlikely to have been available in record stores. Even when the band performed in Sydney and Melbourne in late 1967 and 1968, they introduced audiences to bands such as Traffic (Marks and McIntyre: 186). Secondly, covering songs was both a legitimate artistic exercise and a form of homage. Internationally, from 1967 Vanilla Fudge were known for their interpretations of contemporary songs reworked with extended arrangements that were often related to psychedelic influences. By the end of the 1960s Led Zeppelin took this approach to new heights with their version of 'Dazed and Confused'. For the La De Da's various covers – in particular 'All Along the Watchtower' (the Hendrix version) – became staples serving as showcases for the band's virtuosity. In *The Happy Prince* this is taken to another level with Wilde's tale interpreted through original songs. Recasting a literary form into a pop-rock idiom would be the ultimate 'cover'.

'The Happy Prince': The 1960s and Oscar Wilde in New Zealand

Rodney Charters's *Film Exercise* was a parable for shedding innocence and gaining experience, even if – or maybe because – that experience is a party in dingy student digs. Experience is at the heart of Oscar Wilde's fairy tale, 'The Happy Prince'. As a statue in the city square, The Prince experiences his subjects' vicissitudes causing him, aided by The Swallow, to distribute his adorning jewels and gold flake to the poor and needy. While at the time of contributing to the soundtrack Wilde's tale was simply a shared cultural reference for the band (writing for *The Happy Prince* began in 1967), the film became a vehicle for La De Da's, to develop their artistic capacities following incredible success within the confines of Auckland's emerging pop culture. The film concludes with a La De Da's original recording 'Don't You Stand in My Way', but throughout the music traces the band's intent, from novel interpretation of other musicians' songs to original material that would find its fullest expression in *The Happy Prince*.

While an infatuation with Victorian aesthetics was evident in 1960s pop, from paisley through military braid to Aubrey Beardsley drawings, it may seem incongruous that a 1960s New Zealand rock band would embrace a nineteenth-century Wildean fairy tale to make their artistic statement. Oscar Wilde, however, had a strong presence within the swirling cultural forces of the early 1960s. Wilde was one of the faces all the Beatles agreed should be on the cover of their *Sgt. Pepper's Lonely Hearts Club Band* album (McCartney 2017). More broadly, the revaluation of nature through sensual experience represented in *Film Exercise* would have found favour with Victorian sexual dissidents such as Wilde. Crucially, however, Wilde was an important figure for British and Commonwealth cultural politics in the late 1950s and early 1960s. In Britain, the 1957 Wolfenden Report recommended the government rescind the law that had led to Wilde's imprisonment (effectively that sexual acts between consenting adults should no longer be a criminal offence). The conservative government's subsequent inaction on homosexual law reform encouraged a sincere reconsideration of Wilde. The British Council republished an overview of Wilde and his work by James Laver in 1963 and the same year W. H. Auden wrote a long review of Wilde's life to mark the publication of a new edition of his letters.

Interest in Wilde also increased in the popular arts. In 1960, Micheál MacLiammóir premiered his one-act play, *The Importance of Being Oscar*, which segmented Wilde's life into different periods including 'The Happy Prince' period. That year two sympathetic biographical films on Wilde were released in Britain. The first, *Oscar Wilde* (1960) starring Robert Morley, arrived in New Zealand soon after it was released (*The Press* 1960: 1). The second, more awarded film, *The Trials of Oscar Wilde* (1960) starring English-born Australian actor Peter Finch, was screened regularly in New Zealand cities between 1963 and 1964 (*The Press* 1963: 1; *The Press* 1964a: 29). In 1964, MacLiammóir toured his one-hander in New Zealand where he commented that Auckland theatre goers 'were good to play to and most important, saw the point of all the jokes' (*The Press* 1964b). In that year a BBC programme that argued for a reconsideration of Wilde's ideas and achievements was broadcast on New Zealand Radio. In 1962, the Dorian Society (name checking Wilde's story of Dorian Gray) became the first New Zealand association for homosexual men. In 1967, its members formed the basis of the Wolfenden Association, a society to work for homosexual law reform in New Zealand and which in turn became the New Zealand Homosexual Law Reform Society.[5]

Academic and political interest in Wilde was preceded by the popular engagement with his fairy tales. 'The Happy Prince' had seen a revival in 1940s and 1950s and was consistently a favourite of all Wilde's works (Wood 2002: 157). The fable has inspired nearly fifty musical renditions, from ballet to radio, where its most celebrated version – an Orson Welles and Bing Crosby recording from 1944 – was described by film producer George Miller as 'a story that is so incredibly rich' (*The Treatment* 2022). After receiving the Welles and Crosby recording as a Christmas present as a child, Miller recalled: 'We played "The Happy Prince," my twin brother and I … over and over in that year, almost every night, until it got to the point where we could recite it and perform it almost verbatim' (ibid).[6]

With regard to pop music, Michael Bracewell (1997) has argued that Oscar Wilde was a touchstone for a rebellious 'retreat from Arcady' (7–13) – that mythical idyll of Englishness where rurality and reason meet – evident in twentieth-century British pop music. In his arcane discussion of pop, Bracewell's

Wilde is decidedly historical, despite the 1960s renewal of interest in his relevance for contemporary sexual politics. It is even more ironic – although typical of a discussion mired in Englishness – that Bracewell doesn't notice that since Victorian times imperial settlers had sought Arcady in the colonies. New Zealand was a particular focus of this fantasy to the extent that whole species of animals and plants were transplanted from England to recreate an ideal countryside (Beattie 2014). English migration to New Zealand meant that the English made up more than 40 per cent of foreign-born people, second only to Māori immigration. Until 1974, an English migrant could settle in New Zealand freely, requiring neither visa nor work permit. Bracewell's blindspot exemplifies how 'the homeland' never did give anything away to colonials when it came to popular music. The graveyard of Australian and New Zealand bands was the M1, as they chased headline acts around England while record companies pushed them to cover contemporary English songs – a fate that awaited the La De Da's. Still, Bracewell's observation regarding the allure of Oscar Wilde's work stands. Wilde's commitment to aesthetic experience as a path to spirituality was not out of place in the 1960s youth movement's idea of freedom, as expressed in pop music and its countercultural correlate, psychedelia.

The Welles and Crosby radio version of 'The Happy Prince' was familiar to the La De Da's. Bruce Howard told friends that the recording was a common starting point for the band's introduction to the story (Melanie & Dennis Winters, personal communication).[7] While it was those with the closest relationship to the UK – Howard and Wilson – who championed Wilde's story as inspiration for an album with a consistent story arc, drummer Brett Nielsen also recalled hearing the story while at home as a child listening to the radio. Another New Zealander that I talked to listened to the story broadcast on Sunday mornings and her family acquired an LP recording that they played regularly (Lorraine Sainsbury, personal communication). 'The Happy Prince', she says, was a particularly frightening story. She remembered the terrible feeling every time it reached the point where The Prince's accomplice, The Swallow, dies at the feet at the statue, which then in turn has its leaden heart snap in two. In recognizing the Welles and Crosby performance as particularly accessible to children, George Miller said that when he was growing up the recording provided 'all my sense of story – classic hero myth, all my politics, all the notion of what it is to be empathetic and compassionate, or being cruel; any notion I had of dreaming or aspiring to be in a better place, and yet … confining yourself out of regard for another' (*The Treatment*). There is a certainly a universality to the story of The Prince, who, after years of living well, is made into a glorious gold and bejewelled statue and placed in the town square. Here, confronted with the wretched state of the city's ordinary inhabitants, he sets out to make amends with the help of The Swallow. Yet it also remains a forthrightly Wildean story who never claimed it as a 'children's tale', and it is one of a few fairy tales that feature a male-to-male kiss.

Travelling band

1966 was a breakout year for the band. After going professional as teenagers in December 1965, they had secured the residency at the Platterrack that debuted their tough, creative take on contemporary hit songs, earning them plaudits from Auckland audiences. The band released their first LP in December that year after taking up residency in Eldred Stebbing's Galaxie, a newly renovated venue that boasted the most modern band room in Auckland. By the end of the year, however, the relationship between the band and Stebbing was becoming strained. The studio's insistence that the band record covers and perform in residencies did not fit with the La De Da's ambitions. There had been some exposure beyond Auckland, with national television opportunities on *C'mon* and their performance for the Golden Disc Award but achieving a consistent national profile was difficult. The fragmented nature of national radio – the New Zealand Broadcasting Corporation was effectively made up of city-based stations – and the patchy commitment state broadcasters had to local pop music meant that their music rarely reached audiences outside of Auckland. Income from national sales was crucial to support their developing aspirations to record in England, the mecca for pop stardom. Consequently in 1967 the La De Da's went on the road for their first national tour. They fiercely valued their independence and still worked without a manager but for the tour a road manager was essential. They brought in Hugh Lynn.

As we learned in the previous chapter, Lynn was a key figure in the Auckland scene, providing bouncers and go-go dancers for the local venues. Lynn can't recall why he was asked to be their road manager, but he knew the La De Da's having mixed socially with the band members at the after-parties and venues around Auckland (Lynn). Lynn had valuable experience from being on the road and performing in Aotearoa:

> [My g]randmother was in the circus. And mother was doing shows, not only in Auckland, but outside. As a young boy up to 15, or 16 years old, I'd travelled with them […] My mother said, you know, that you've got a responsibility as an artist

to get on stage and do your very best and you can't stop. You've got to keep going. So, I came with that sort of attitude and philosophy … To get the band on stage, and to do our rehearsals, and that sort of thing was fairly familiar to me.

While he recalls the band as being very professional, his organizational skills and contacts proved valuable in other ways. Towards the end of the tour the band was owed money from a promoter and Lynn had to call on the 'brothers' in Auckland:

We didn't sign contracts or anything [and] we got into difficulties with the promoter who stopped paying us. The deal was that we got the money each night, but he stopped paying us for about three gigs in Whangamatā [just south of Auckland, virtually the last gig of the tour]. I rang some of my security […] because he was starting to threaten us. I think about 15 of my men came down there and we took over the dance and I got the money that was owing to us. There was some arguments there, but no physicality.

Without the grind of a club residency and with Lynn trusted to take care of the logistics, the band had the opportunity to consider their next move in music.

Songs that would eventually form part of *The Happy Prince* began to emerge on this tour. New Zealand music historian Grant Gillanders wrote that the ideas took shape as the band travelled, prompted in part by Bruce Howard's chance find of a new instrument:

Stopping off at an unknown small town for a pie and pit-stop, Howard noticed a harmonium in a second-hand shop window. The group's already laden van had to be re-arranged to accommodate Howard's new purchase […]

> Howard spent the idle hours on the road experimenting with the new sounds the harmonium offered and thus was born their concept album, *The Happy Prince*.
>
> (Gillanders 2021)

Brett Nielsen recalled: 'He was playing it the whole time while we're driving. And [...] that's the first I recall of that project being started.' The 'birthing story' is one of the many myths that has accreted to the legend of the La De Da's *The Happy Prince*. Australian music journalist Jeff Jenkins (2023) would later claim that 'by mid-1967, Wilson and Howard had written half of the rock opera, and The La De Da's were playing four of the songs live: Come and Fly with Me, Civic Pride, Winter Song and Swallow, Little Swallow'. Kevin Borich reflected that initially the story was considered a vehicle for songwriting:

> It was the idea of the story more so than the tag of what's called [a] concept album ... It's a template for a start, to write about the notion of the story. It is a great door to open [...] it gives you a good reason to sort of craft the songs, to go with the emotion of the circumstance.

The story of 'The Happy Prince' effectively provided the band with an approach that could raise the artistic and emotional level of their songwriting at a time when literature and art were becoming important to pop music.

Pop/Culture

Album-based rock music began to take a distinct cultural turn in the mid-1960s. There was no general commitment to a conceptual form for long play recording: an album could simply be a collection of tracks or it could consist of stylistically and lyrically linked songs. At the same time, literary figures were becoming influential in contemporary songwriting and popular music, which was increasingly being called on to 'say *something*'. The 1965 International Poetry Incarnation at Albert Hall in London – organized in some measure by expatriate Kiwi, John Esam (Bollinger: 80–2) – provided a forum by which poets, songwriters, dope smokers and activists could recognize their commonalities. Many see this as the beginning of the counterculture. In New Zealand writing by American Beats, such as Kerouac's *On the Road* (1957), was disseminated through cheap paperback versions (Bollinger: 122). Allen Ginsberg's 'Howl' (first published in 1956) had become an important cultural text. A decade after its publication and the blow struck for free expression when its banned status was overturned in the United States, poet Jeffrey Paparoa Holman encountered the profanity in *Howl and Other Poems* when it was read aloud in his university lecture (2020). Singer Bob Dylan was breaking down the boundaries between poetry and pop. Dylan's fraternisation with the Beats in San Francisco at the end of 1965 marked the "bridging of two cultural movements" according to Simon Warner (2013: 1). Dylan had already established himself as a catalyst by turning The Beatles onto marijuana a year earlier, while drug culture's contribution to creativity was becoming notorious in the hands of William S. Burroughs – the Beat author with arguably the most influence on popular music (Rae 2020). Dylan had skipped New Zealand on his 1966 world tour, but in Melbourne he was contacted and befriended by poet, cultural critic and Beat aficionado, Adrian Rawlins. During the mid-1960s, as the album form became increasingly malleable, understanding popular music as art would often be mediated by drugs.

From 1965, the British press had begun making connections between rock, art and opera. The Who – particularly Pete Townsend aided and abetted by the band's manager Kit Lambert – had taken to linking their music to the pop art movement. When the single 'Anyway, Anyhow, Anywhere' was released in June 1965, Lambert argued it linked music to art through its creative studio production: 'Jet planes, emergency signals, city traffic. What more do you want without going to the sound effects library? It's going to be very difficult to put pop art principles into lyrics' (Green 1965). In December 1966 *Melody Maker* referred to The Who's track 'A Quick One While He's Away' as a 'miniature pop opera' (Welch 1966) while Townsend declared 'we stand for pop art clothes, pop art music and pop art behavior' (Stanfield 2017). By 1967, The Beatles used the LP form to stage a connected – if not cohesive – musical arts project. From cover art, through sleeve lyrics to the closing track, the counterculture had its first major artistic statement – and a number one best seller: *Sgt. Pepper's Lonely Hearts Club Band*. The Who's ambition to link songs and ideas later reached its zenith with *Tommy* (1969): pop music in an opera format with Townshend's Indian guru, Meher Baba, listed as the concept's avatar. While the La De Da's own album was released months before *Tommy*, this was the context within which their ideas for *The Happy Prince* developed.

Conclusion

The La De Da's relied on the resources of Eldred Stebbing. He was not officially their manager, but the band recorded in his production facilities, and since signing on as a house band at Galaxie, they were even more tightly within his orbit.

Stebbing had a history of exploiting bands and then moving on. He saw success with Ray Columbus and the Invaders, but after the hit phenomenon of 'She's a Mod' could not be repeated, the band found money increasingly tight under Stebbing's management and soon disbanded. Even while he continued to manage them, Stebbings had already brought in the Pleazers from Australia, in an attempt to find a viable economic replacement. Soon they joined Galaxie but were then replaced by the new kids on the block, the La De Da's. By the end of 1966, Stebbing was beginning to tire of the La De Da's too. This made the band's tour of the north and south islands even more important as it provided them with an independent source of income. In the future, successful tours of New Zealand allowed them to continue to explore their own ambitions in music. Still, the culture of money and how it provided access to resources would bedevil the band's aspirations with regard to *The Happy Prince*.

Gillanders and Welsh (142) note that Eldred Stebbing admired the success of Ivan Dayman in Australia, who by 1966 had built a pop entertainment empire. Beginning in Adelaide in December 1959 by promoting dances under the banner of the Adelaide Swing Shows, Dayman was contracted to find young performers for the local *Teentime* television programme. He developed interests in the emerging Melbourne suburban dance scene, and on weekends he drove nine hours to that city from Adelaide, often accompanied by *Teentime* performers who would play at venues he leased on the weekend. Dayman eventually set up Cloudland in Brisbane, taking with him a Melbourne band, The Bluejays, to back his growing list of singers, many of whom were New Zealanders who had come to Australia looking for career opportunities. At one point Dayman's booking roster listed Toni Williams (Cook Islands), the

Hi-Liners (Maori showband) and Ja-Ar – John Rowles (North Island, Bay of Plenty). New Zealand band The Librettos backed for Dayman's solo acts when they toured. When Dayman formed the Sunshine label as an independent off-shoot of Sydney-based distribution and recording company Festival, he had a regional and capital city circuit of venues with a stable of performers that he managed. Through his Bowl Booking Bureau, he could book them into his clubs or pull them into Festival's Sydney studio facilities to record covers of hit songs for Sunshine. It was the first integrated entertainment group in Australian pop music. In Sydney Dayman's representative was Graham Dent, the estranged husband Diana Dent, founder of The Casual Shop.

In the late 1960s, Dent was one of Dayman's key lieutenants. He became an important link for Eldred Stebbing into Dayman's network. Dent had cut his teeth in late 1950s rock 'n' roll. As an Auckland assistant theatre manager, he had contributed to the success of Bill Haley's film *Rock Around the Clock* (1956) and later, in 1958, convinced his employer – the Kerridge Organisation – to use their north island chain of cinemas for a rock 'n' roll tour. The singer he toured with was Johnny Devlin, whose band, the Devils, was put together by pianist Claude Papesch. Dent became known as a master of the stunt. He briefly worked with Harry M. Miller in Auckland in the early 1960s (Miller 1983: 77) before managing Max Merritt and the Meteors tour to Australia in December 1964. Dent organized a four-week cabaret residency at the Rex Hotel in Kings Cross – which also hosted the Maori showband The Quin Tikis – and a television appearance on Johnny O'Keefe's *Sing Sing Sing*. By early 1967, however, Dent's cabaret act aspirations for the band ended when a cruise he booked them on led to the defection of several band members and he and Merritt parted ways.[8]

At this time Dent was already working for the booking and promotion arm of Dayman's organisation in Sydney (Brown 2018: 78–9). Dent maintained his New Zealand connections, including with Eldred Stebbing, for whom he became a kind of fixer. When Stebbing wanted to offload The Pleazers, he told them Dent would cover their arrangements in Sydney and sent them there. When the band arrived, in August 1966, they were told they had been expected weeks earlier and the promised performance work was no longer available (Gilmore 1995: 54). Later, when the La De Da's were creating issues for Stebbing, with their insistence on recording original material, they were also passed onto Dayman's network in Sydney with disastrous results.

3   *Find Us a Way*

Sin City/Sydney

In April 1965, Eldred Stebbing was in Sydney scouting for new talent to replace Ray Columbus and the Invaders, when he was introduced to The Pleazers. The young band had a residency at the Italian Club on Oxford St in Darlinghurst but had initially hailed from Brisbane (although the two lead singers were Kiwis). They had travelled south, to Sydney, the capital of the state of New South Wales (NSW), to find their fortune but got more than they bargained for. Drummer, Denis Gilmore wrote: 'Only six months before in Brisbane I was a very naïve 20-year-old who didn't have a steady girlfriend, didn't smoke, drink or take drugs. The six months later I was 21 (supposedly an adult) living in Sydney, sharing a house with four prostitutes, and played [*sic*] in night clubs run by the Mafia' (Gilmore 1995: 28). Sydney had a reputation for being a seedy city, but by the time the La De Da's arrived in May 1967, things had got a whole lot worse.

Robert Askin, elected Premier of New South Wales in 1965, had presided over an unprecedented expansion of corruption and crime, from illegal gambling and prostitution in Darlinghurst and Kings Cross to the entertainment industry.[1] Sydney had earned the moniker of 'sin city' and, with its licensed clubs and hotels and commercial media, it was a very different city to Auckland. Graham Dent claimed it was the Sydney mafia that made him decide to move out of the music industry and return to New Zealand (Dent 1992: T3). In the late 1960s

Sydney was beginning a period of intense redevelopment that impacted on music and counter-culture venues. Between January and October 1968, the experimental theatre space 10 Cunningham St, described as 'the heart of the underground' (McIntyre: 119) shared a laneway with Chequers, the Wong family's premier nightclub venue until city regulations shut it down (the Sydney City Archives have it listed as an 'unlicensed youth cabaret' (City of Sydney)). Juno Gemes, a Cunningham St founder, later said: 'After six months the people who owned Chequers, the City Fathers, the police and all the powers in the city wanted us closed down' (McIntyre: 121). If you had the muscle, this city could be reshaped as easily as the sandstone on which it had been founded.

The La De Da's arrived in the autumn of 1967 and set themselves up in cheap digs in Kings Cross. The locality drew its name from being at the crossroad. From the east to the west, one road led from the city's chic eastern suburbs to the CBD. The other, running north to south, took you from the docks at Woolloomooloo and into seedy Darlinghurst. Straddling these urban arteries, the Cross in the 1960s was congested, noisy and grubby. It showed its best side at night, under neon, when the grime was not obvious. The band's digs were within walking distance of venues in the precinct. Around the Cross at this time building was underway for new nightclubs and venues that would reshape the city. The iconic Surf City – once a beachhead for Ray Columbus and the Invaders attack on Sydney's pop charts – had closed a year earlier. Along with the adjacent Kings Cross theatre it made way for the fourteen-storey Crest Hotel, which was opened in October 1967. Meanwhile, the former manager of Surf City – bookmaker and entrepreneur, John Harrigan – paid $50,000 for a fit-out of the new Whiskey-a-Go-Go in nearby William Street, where he partnered with

Denis Wong (on the Wong family see Hickie 1985: 445–7). From the Cross, you could also walk to Castlereagh Street, which at the time housed many of the city's booking agencies, venues and studios including EMI's 301 studio – named due to its location in the street. At the top of the Castlereagh Street, near Central Station, stood the Tivoli Theatre. Travelling towards the harbour, The Prince Edward, originally Australia's 'cathedral of motion pictures' (*Sydney Mail* 1928), was just past King St. At 212 Castlereagh Street the Methodist Mission hosted Teenage Cabaret, established to provide a safe entertainment venue for youth in a city where violence was all too common (Alexander 1967; Gambie & Suich 1967). Further on at Martin Place, just before the road becomes Bligh St and dips towards the ferry terminals, was the magnificent Australia Hotel, which, in 1968, was bought by an insurance company who demolished it a few years later and replaced with a sixty-seven-floor skyscraper.

Ivan Dayman's Sydney Bowl nightclub was in a basement in Castlereagh St, near the corner of Park St, and above it was the Bowl Booking Bureau. This and other similar agencies were key to getting gigs in the city. The Bowl Booking Bureau was run by Lonnie Lee, a former rocker who had turned to management. Lee remembered the La De Da's arrival in Sydney as they came with the reputation of 'a very, very good band musically but, they didn't have any drawing capacity, they were very, very new' (Lee). Attempting to become known, the La De Da's pasted posters on William St declaring 'The La De Da's have arrived' (Borich). They got a write-up in the main Sunday newspaper where Normie Rowe predicted they would 'build into something very big' (*Sun-Herald* 1967a: 98). A few days after arriving in Sydney the band were supporting The Easybeats on the second leg of their Australian homecoming tour. The Easybeats had returned triumphantly from overseas engagements and played Sydney earlier in May. They used Dayman's booking agency for domestic tours. When on their way across to Perth, they transited through Sydney again and held an initially unscheduled afternoon show at The Stadium, an old boxing ring with a rotating stage that was just below the Cross at Rushcutters Bay. The La De Da's were in the right place at the right time and were signed up as supports.

In May 1967, when the band arrived in Australia, LSD was not prohibited. (For more on LSD in the 1960s see: **https://bloomsbury.pub/the-happy-prince/psychedelia**). Kevin Borich recalls taking the drug in laced sugar cubes: 'We were never dropping LSD and going to a party. We were either in a space whereby we wouldn't be interrupted [...] listening to Hendrix or Traffic. We loved Steve Winwood. [Later] we were playing a lot of covers over here [Australia] and then extending those songs for our improvisation skills' (Borich). As I discussed in the previous chapter, LSD and its cultural expression – psychedelia – were considered legitimate ways to remove oneself from the corruption of the mainstream society and to transcend Western reasoning. In May 1967 (when the La De Da's arrived in Sydney), it was the focus of a commercial television documentary which demonstrated both a good trip and a bad trip for the viewers at home (McIntyre: 65). LSD was so accepted in certain circles that in July that year Billy Thorpe announced on a TV pop programme, the *Go!! Show*, that he had been commissioned by a magazine to 'take a trip' on LSD and have his thoughts published (*The Age* 1967: 3). His comments caused a furore with conservative commentators. Despite further explanation that he had organized medical supervision as a safeguard, he was branded irresponsible and threatened with arrest (*The Age* 1967) even though he was not breaking any laws by taking LSD. Just days after his announcement, Thorpie backed down, saying he was not condoning 'tripping' (*Sydney Morning Herald* 1967: 12). While this incident demonstrated resistance to the counterculture breaking out of its underground existence, bands continued to engage with psychedelia as experimentation. Throughout 1967, *Go-Set*, a music newspaper that had been established in Melbourne a year earlier, reported that various performers, from Paul McCartney through Glenn Shorrock (The Twilights) to Mama Cass had said they had experienced LSD or they wanted to do so. Darlinghurst's Cell Block Theatre had shown an interest in new media art from 1966 when it hosted the visual artist and musician Lindsay Bourke's debut solo exhibition of sound and light mixed media. In August 1967, the theatre was home to Jazz Happenings billed as 'The World's First Psychedelic Jazz Concert' (Organ 2019). In September, the Wayside Chapel Theatre – a relatively new and innovative venue established by the urban Methodist Wesley Mission to reach out to young people – hosted two evenings of experimental music and image from young composer John Terry. Terry performed electric organ and piano accompanied by actuality or found sound, abstract projector slides and hand-coloured film presenting a 'new sort of contemporary music … with a series of shattering visual images' (*Sun Herald* 1967b: 104). The Wayside ran Teenage Cabaret, with its own teenage host, Jim Towers, presenting psychedelic inspired local bands such as Lotus.

By the end the year state laws were introduced restricting importation and use of LSD in New South Wales and Victoria, which covered Australia's two largest cities (Sydney and

Melbourne respectively). Thus began the proscription of the drug even while it continued to be widely used, especially amongst US soldiers serving in Vietnam, who from October 1967 could visit Sydney on official 'rest & recreation' (R&R) tours. It was in the La De Da's second incarnation as a band, when the returned to Sydney in 1968, that they developed their reputation for psychedelic music. As late as July 1970, they participated in an 'Acid Test' at Sydney's Trocadero nightclub, which was billed as 'an environmental recreation of the L.S.D. experience' (*Sydney Morning Herald* 1970: 19). In 1967, however, at the beginning of their initial stay in Australia, the band had to confront the new conditions they found in Sydney.

After The Easybeats show, the La De Da's secured a week-long residency at DJ Ward 'Pally' Austin's Jungle discotheque in York St in the city. Austin was one of several players from commercial radio in the Australian music industry. For the La De Da's the impact of this kind of radio and the personalities it generated was new. The staid NZBC presenters were the antithesis of the commercial Sydney DJs who had a stranglehold on music in the city. While there was nothing that smacked of the US payola scandal that broke in 1960, the Sydney DJs were highly competitive with a good understanding of their star-making power. Newspaper proprietors had bought into the commercial radio industry in the 1950s and each paper had relationships with specific broadcasters.[2] Promoters took to shaping performers into the kind of deal they believed would sell on commercial radio. On arrival in Sydney, the La De Da's found that Dayman's handlers had specific plans for them. John Dix wrote: 'Demanding the boys clean up their image … Jimmy Murta [Dayman's employee] threw himself into the assignment arranging radio and press interviews, and $3,000 worth of publicity photos.' Dayman also arranged for the band to perform at his venue in Brisbane.

Dayman's expensive pitch was aimed squarely at the teenage market (Dix 1988: 69). In an incredible puff piece on their arrival in Sydney 'padding around the airport in the hand-stitched calf skin boots' (Pattersen 1967), their ages were dropped by several years. This emphasis was unsettling for a band that had begun to move away from a teenage image. It did not hit the mark with Australian audiences either. The group's single 'Hey Baby!' had been released in Sydney to coincide with their arrival. While it was rocketing up the charts in New Zealand, where it became their biggest seller yet, it did not enter the charts in Sydney or Melbourne, demonstrating the difference between the music markets in each country. The follow-up single 'All-Purpose Low' did worse. Both singles received lowly ratings in the influential Melbourne-based music paper *Go-Set* with 'All-Purpose Low' receiving the lowest possible score from their 'pop panel' (*Go Set* 1967d: 2). Later the song received a ban by Australian radio stations and required re-recording before it was suitable for Australian broadcasts (*Billboard* 1967; *Go Set* 1967e: 18).

New Zealanders across 'the Ditch'

As the La De Da's struggled to sustain a profile after their arrival in Sydney, the expatriate Kiwi community, that included Jackie Holme and Bobi Nicholas, helped them settle in. Holme, who had cut Dinah Lee's distinctive bob in the back room of The Casual Shop boutique in Auckland in 1964, was living with Billy

Thorpe at the time of his dalliance with acid evangelism. She had achieved success as a model working in London before returning to Sydney in late 1965. Holme had remained in contact with Bobi Nicholas (See Figure 3.1), who had again taken up residence in Sydney and managed The Casual Shop's Australian boutique, where all the clothes were one-off creations made in New Zealand. When Dinah Lee moved to Sydney permanently to consolidate her growing stardom, Nicholas was employed as her private secretary and road manager (Cartwright 2013). Holme, Billy Thorpe, Nicholas and Lee all resided in the same apartment block Rushcutters Bay, the chic eastern harbourside suburb just below the Cross. Max Merritt had also lived there (with Jackie) during his cabaret period, performing at nearby Rex Hotel. Nicholas recalls meeting the La De Da's as a band for the first time when they performed with Dinah Lee in Brisbane at Ivan Dayman's Cloudland, a huge venue that had rooms for performers:

> [Ivan] would put the groups up in this biggish … apartment and we stayed with the La De Da's. That's really where I got to meet the La De Da's … and Bruce, he was my favourite. [We were] quite close because he was from the north shore in Auckland and we got along really well.
>
> (Petch)

Nicholas and Lee later took Kevin Borich and former Invaders guitarist Dave Russell to see The Shadows – Borich was a fan – when they had a residency at Chequers nightclub in Sydney (Petch).

Sydney had become the favoured home for entertainers and cultural hipsters from Aotearoa living 'across the ditch' as the Tasman Sea was affectionately known. Some performers looked to emulate Ray Columbus and the Invaders' success with 'She's a Mod', while others were attracted by the constant work and excitement of a larger city. By this time New Zealand band, The Librettos, had become Ivan Dayman's house band and they regularly toured with his singers to Sydney and other parts of Australia. The Australian harbour city was a destination of choice for many Kiwis. Along with Max Merritt, there were Māori showbands playing at the Rex Hotel, while others took

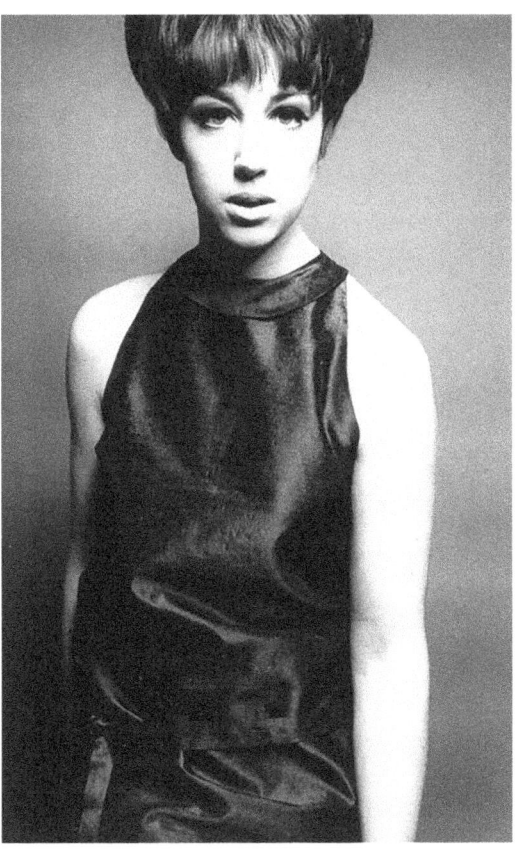

Figure 3.1 *Bobi Nicholas. Bobi Petch Collection.*

steady jobs. Johnny Devlin became artists and repertoire (A&R) manager for RCA in Sydney. In 1966, Rod Coe took a twelve-month sabbatical from his job in the New Zealand Broadcasting Corporation and came to Sydney to join a band that had a two-nights-a-week residency at John & Charleys, a discotheque above the Bourbon and Beefsteak restaurant in Kings Cross. His 'day jobs' included work at the fashionable In-Shop on Hunter Street in the CBD while living at the Cross:

> In those days, people used to go out a lot and you'd get the same sort of crowds on Friday and Saturday night. People just had a great time. […] We were living in Kings Cross, in a flat with a couple of the bandmates. And that was a very exciting place to be. You felt like it was the centre of Sydney. […] It was pretty amazing to me: the luxury of Vaucluse [an eastern suburb close to the Cross] compared to people on the street in Redfern [inner city low rent suburb]. Wow, I've never seen anything like that sort of extreme before.
>
> (Coe)

Expatriate Britisher and number-one New Zealand band fan John Dix came to Sydney to write about the Aotearoa musical exports in the city for *Go Set*:

> It seemed that every major Australian band had one Kiwi in the line-up: Johnny Dick (Doug Parkinson In Focus), Teddy Toi (Wild Cherries), Mike Rudd (Party Machine) … the raw roar of Leo De Castro, Pete Williams fronting The Groove, guns-for-hire like Claude Papesch, Bruno Lawrence and Tim Piper; Ricky May redefining Australian jazz vocals and the velvety tones of Rim D Paul on the supper club circuit.
>
> (2014a; see also 2014b)

Within Holme and Nicholas's social set, and with these women's connections to the Sydney music industry, the boys from the La De Da's at least felt they had a toehold in that chaotic city.

Melbourne had its own style as Nicholas found out: 'My first official job with Dinah Lee was to accompany her to Melbourne, which was such a different scene than Sydney's club/pub/RSL one. Melbourne had a young dance scene to perform to.' Later, as Melbourne developed a pop industry with well-appointed inner-city discotheques, excellent production facilities (such as Armstrong's studio) and dedicated pop media, the Meteors and other Kiwi bands such as Larry's Rebel based themselves there, along with Australian bands from all over the country (Homan et al. 2021). When the La De Da's arrived in Sydney in May 1967, Max Merritt had recently returned from the ill-fated Pacific cruise his manager Graham Dent had booked for his band. He had gathered a new band of rock and former jazz players to take on the soul direction he wanted to move in and took off south to Melbourne. It was a shock to the New Zealand expatriates and musicians to hear that Merritt's new band was involved in a terrible accident in June that year. A woman in the other car was killed and the band, apart from guitarist John 'Yuk' Harrison, were left with serious injuries. It would be another year before the Meteors were back on stage. Melbourne, as I discuss below, would also see a 'crash' of sorts for La De Da's, which proved a breaking point of the band's solidarity.

The initial *Happy Prince* recording in Sydney

Earlier, I mentioned how the influence of handlers and radio personalities was disconcerting for the band on their arrival in Sydney. Even more concerning were problems the band encountered with recording the album they had begun writing, *The Happy Prince*. They had worked up at least one song, 'Come and Fly with Me', that they were looking to record in Sydney with Ivan Dayman's contacts and Eldred Stebbing's support. Here their timing was not good. An acrimonious financial dispute had engulfed Dayman's Sunshine label, which led to an inexperienced producer at the helm when the band finally got into a studio. While this episode is likely to have soured their initial visit to Sydney, it would not be the last nor the least disappointing of the band's failed attempts to record in Australia. The 'lost sessions' of *The Happy Prince* would become the stuff of legend.

The band planned to put down 'Come and Fly with Me' as a single from the songs they had begun to create using the structure of Wilde's story. Stebbing had made arrangements to record with Dayman's Sunshine label which was distributed by Festival Records, the largest and most influential recording company in Australia.[3] Festival had studios in Sydney which they leased to the labels that they distributed, but those studios were old and dilapidated. Festival was already planning to move their recording from the old building in Harris St further down towards the harbour to a new building on Pyrmont St. These new premises would be constructed with modern acoustical design and incorporate multitracking facilities, but they were not yet ready when the La De Da's recorded. Dayman's company booked the band into the old studios where 'techniques were still primitive and limited to one-track recording on an old Ampex tape machine. To pick up each member of [a] band, microphones were placed on cabinets, chairs or piles of books' (Cox 2001: 29). While the band was used to innovation and compromise from working out of

Stebbing's home-based Zodiac studios, these conditions must have been a shock. Missing the chance to record in a new modern studio was, however, just one aspect of bad timing for the band's 1967 Sunshine sessions.

At the end of 1966, just prior to the La De Da's landing in Sydney, Ivan Dayman's empire was in an increasingly precarious financial situation. Sunshine Records, with Festival as the major creditor, was the asset that he was prepared to let go. During 1966, Dayman began to refuse to pay Festival's studio expenses as he focused on his performers and clubs. Dayman had funded Normie Rowe and his band on an expensive foray to England for performances and recording, with little financial success to show for it. Back in Australia, Pat Aulton was employed by Sunshine for its recording arrangements with Festival. Despite the conditions at Festival's Harris St studios, he produced some of Australia's finest beat band recordings including classic sessions with The Wild Cherries. As Sunshine's financial matters worsened in late 1966, Aulton took the fall and creditors took most of his possessions (Brown: 26). Later, after the dust from the financial collapse had settled, Aulton went on to be the in-house producer at Festival and continued to be esteemed by musicians that worked with him. He had a significant impact on Australian pop music. In the meantime, as Aulton sorted out the financial problems Dayman's collapse had left him with, Festival continued to lease their old studios to Sunshine. Steve Neale was brought in to replace Aulton as the label's house producer. While an experienced musician, having played in Brisbane band The Planets for some time, Neale was a novice producer. The La De Da's did not have good rapport with Neale and they were frustrated with both the process and the conditions. The band walked out before the session was completed. Drummer Brett Nielsen recalled:

'I have a strong memory of being in the studio in Sydney. 'Come and Fly with Me' [eventually the single released from *The Happy Prince* recordings in 1969]. It was only one track. And I remember it being very unsatisfactory. There was bickering and, I don't know. It didn't seem that we got anything out of it'.

This would be the only attempt at recording *The Happy Prince* for Nielsen. By the time of the La De Da's second visit to Sydney in 1968, he had quit the band.

Melbourne

While the studio experience was frustrating, for Nielsen the nadir of his time with the band had come earlier during the band's gruelling visit to Melbourne in August and September. Where their Sydney residencies were based around inner city venues, the Melbourne scene was very different. Suburban dances (sometimes managed by police or church services to provide youth activities), discos and local town halls were important venues and a band would often do three shows a day beginning in an outer suburban club then gradually, gear in tow, finish with a late-night gig at an inner-city venue. As Nielsen recalls: 'We'd start in the outer suburbs, and we do one there in a town hall or something, and bottles and stuff thrown at us. And then you'd come back in more towards town.' That August was particularly cold with the lowest temperature of the year, just over 1°C (34°F) recorded that month. The band bunked in a room in a large house rented by compatriots Max Merritt and the Meteors, who were recovering from their horrific car accident that had occurred just weeks earlier. While the physical exertion in such conditions was exhausting, it was the impact of psychotropic substances that tested the drummer's commitment.

On August 10, The Beatles' new album *Sgt. Peppers' Lonely Hearts Club Band* was released in Australia. The album received maximum exposure. EMI (Australia) sponsored a Beatles Week, commencing 31 July, where the album was promoted by record stores and nationwide, through TV, radio and newspapers campaigns (*I am the Platypus*). Nielsen recalls:

> We arrived [in Melbourne], basically on the eve of *Sgt. Pepper's* … coming out. And that seemed to be the catalyst to launch everyone, except me, into using LSD … And I remember, there's a huge room [for] the five of us, all of us were [living] in that room. Bruce had rye bread on every flat surface trying to grow mould [to produce ergot, a psychoactive fungus]. But that was hell for me. The roadie would arrive, and it would just get worse and worse as evening went on. We, the roadie and me, would do everything, we'd do all the lifting, they were off their faces. I remember one night Kevin even couldn't even plug his amp in and I had to do it for him.

A flick through *Go Set* for this period confirms Nielsen's sense that there was a shift in the profile of psychedelic styles and events. First out of the blocks with psychedelic-style graphics in *Go Set* was the Ginza nightclub. Opened in late June, 1967, it was described in an archly satiric comment in *The Bulletin* (1967) as the city's first 'genuine psychedelic discotheque' (5). Ginza is one of the only venues that did not advertise specific bands: instead, its tagline was '[t]he only discotheque where the place is bigger than the bands' (*Go Set* 1967a: 17). The entrepreneurs behind Ginza – apparently three Monash University students (*The Bulletin* 1967) – engaged artist and designer Frank Eidlitz to style the interior of the venue. In 1966, Eidlitz had received a Churchill fellowship. He spent a year in the United States working with visual artist György Kepes and returned as an apostle of psychedelia as the next big art movement (*The Bulletin* op cit; *Australian Graphic Design*). But if Eidlitz was ahead of the curve, in a couple of months others caught up. In August, the suburban Coburg Town Hall dance, branded 'Swingers', pushed their new facility to cater for a new crowd: '"Swingers" apologises if you were too crowded last Saturday night, but this Saturday we open the Psychedelic love-in balcony for you to gaze down in supreme comfort upon guest villains, the Twilights' (*Go Set* 1967b: 22). Numerous of other Melbourne venues adopted references to psychedelic experiences in advertising, while a new coffee lounge in Carlton, called Love-In, opened to cater to the tuned-in and freaked-out as 'the first psychedelic place of its kind in Australia, with décor that had to be seen to be believed' and a store next door that sold 'hippie gear … direct from New York and Haight Ashbury (home of the American flower children)' (*Go Set* 1967c: 6). While consuming psychedelia did not always mean taking LSD, it was an environment where being experienced through acid was readily accepted.

The poet

Adrian Rawlins would have supported the Carlton 'Love-in's' commitment to a range of entertainment "from guest groups' records, films, to poetry readings" (*Go Set* 1967c) but he would have no need for the "hippie gear" on sale there. Rawlins always was hip, by his own account. In 1994, then in his mid fifties Rawlins reflected: 'My life is taking much the course that …

came into my mind in these little morning reveries between the ages of four and a half and seven or eight' (National Library of Australia 1994). A precocious child, Rawlins was initially educated at the alternative bush school, Koornong, outside Melbourne at Warrandyte. His art teacher was Danila Vassilieff, the Russian-born Australian artist who has been called the "father of Australian modernism" (Bojic 2007). While he later attended traditional schooling, it did not suit Rawlins. In 1952, when Adrian was thirteen years old, his father died. At sixteen he left school for clerical work. At the same time, he was attending Fellowship of Australian Writer's meetings and was a regular at Clifton Hocking's record store, Thomas's in Bourke Street. Despite being underage he could be found in the Swanston Family Hotel back bar, a home of Melbourne's bohemians, botting cigarettes off the like of Barry Humphries, Germaine Greer and Clifton Pugh. A restless soul, Rawlins never felt bound by the conventions of contemporary society. His education continued at the house of lawyer, writer and communist Leo Cash, who shared with him copies of *Twenty First Century* (1955–7), published in Australia by anarchist and poet Harry Hooton. Here he encountered the American Beat poets. Rawlins was profoundly influenced by Ginsberg's 'Howl' and would later recite it in Melbourne and Sydney performances. For Rawlins, the Beats spoke to him in his time. In an unpublished memoir, 'Poetry and Jazz "beat" the rap', he recalled:

> I encountered the American Beat school in 1958 in an English anthology of 'angry young men' and their American counterparts. To me at that time, 17 … the English writing still seemed contrived and artificial … still part of the 'official' universe – of language, attitude and assumption … The Beat writing, on the other hand knocked me over precisely because it dealt with a social, physical and moral milieu

synonymous with the one I was inhabiting … So when I read, either in 1958 or 9 of the trial of Ginsberg on a charge of obscenity and pornographic publication, I was vitally interested.

The moral guardianship of the state in Australia at this time cannot be overestimated. It would be another decade before the Sydney Film Festival was allowed to present uncensored international films. The success of Ginsberg's defence demonstrated a world in flux.

Rawlins soon fell in with artists and promoters such as Ian Sime, a Second World War veteran who had lived in Japan, and Kym Bonython, who maintained an important gallery in Sydney but is best known both as a speed racer and for his broadcasts and promotion of jazz. In 1964, twenty-five-year-old Rawlins attended the Ray Charles concerts in Melbourne with Bonython who had secured the jazz great's first Australian tour. By this time Rawlins was becoming well-known as a bon vivant and a celebrated critic. His break had come early in 1960 after he had attended the 14th Convention of Australian Jazz in the country town of Cootamundra in December 1959. His reports on the Convention in *The Observer* (Sydney) led to further commissions. That journal was in the process of merging with *The Bulletin*, then Australia's most well-known liberal journal on culture and politics. Initially Rawlins was disappointed to find *The Observer* was not printing his articles until, as he recounted, an acquaintance said to him: "'Oh I see you're writing for *The Bulletin* now … ". And of course, then I became the bright young thing of everybody in the Fellowship of Australian Writers' (National Library of Australia 1994). On his return to Melbourne from Cootamundra, Rawlins and his friend Volfga Mooki Hermon established weekly jazz and poetry performances at

The Fat Black Pussycat, a Melbourne bohemian venue. In the daytime it doubled as a rehearsal room for bands and later, it emerged as an early rhythm and blues venue hosting The Wild Cherries, whose drummer, Keith Barber, later joined the La De Da's and recorded *The Happy Prince*. When the art critic for *The Age*, Melbourne's most prestigious daily, passed away in 1962 twenty-three-year-old Rawlins applied for the appointment, but he was overlooked. He continued to write for marginal popular news journals, including the *Jewish News*, student newspapers such as *Farrago* (Monash University) and *Catalyst* (RMIT), but most importantly he wrote record reviews for the Sydney-based music journal, *Music Maker*, where he made money from selling both the reviews and the records (National Library Australia 1994). While Rawlins continued to think of himself as a poet, it was through his cultural journalism that he developed a reputation as an innovator and came to befriend Bob Dylan.

In September 1963, when Pete Seeger toured Australia, Rawlins attended his concerts and was at his press conference as a writer for *Music Maker*. An indefatigable networker to whom it was hard to say no, Rawlins, with other journalists, found himself at dinner with Seeger, who was discussing a poet, Bobby, who had stopped writing. A few days later when at his concert Seeger sang a song by Bobby, 'A Hard Rain's A- Gonna Fall', Rawlins recalled: 'I found to my mind a degree of poetry equal to Elliot at his best or to Lorca (National Library of Australia 1994).' Later that year, on a visit to Sydney he encountered Dylan's recent album, likely to be *The Freewheelin' Bob Dylan*, which had 'A Hard Rain's A- Gonna Fall' as well as 'Blowin' in the Wind' and 'Masters of War'. (In his oral history Rawlins says he listened to Dylan's third album, which was *The Times They Are a'Changin*, but that was not released until February 1964 and unlikely to have made it to Australia until much later that year.) Three years later in 1966, with Dylan scheduled to tour Australia Rawlins convinced the editor of *The Age*'s entertainment guide to print an article he had written. Called '10 Statements on Dylan', it was in the poetic style of the later Paul Eluard (National Library of Australia 1994; Rawlins 1966a). Rawlins attended Dylan's press conference, again for *Music Maker*, and he would later say he experienced a form of mystical awakening. He became aware that popular music could be a vehicle for spiritual renewal, a view he expressed in the journal *Arena* in 1966:

> The Beatles and The Rolling Stones and Dylan are evidence of a new sort of spirit arising in human beings that will bring about the communist utopia […]. And I thought that was pretty much the case. And after having written that article (See Rawlins 1966b) … I felt totally at ease, as though I really had connected with my true destiny.
>
> (National Library of Australia 1994)

It was around this time that Rawlins began to associate himself with the teachings of Meher Baba, a relationship he would continue throughout his life. Baba taught that the goal of all beings was to gain consciousness of their own divinity. His philosophy was an amalgam of various Indian thought and has been said 'to helped inspire Laing's "anti-psychiatry" in the 1960s' (Sovatsky 2004).

Rawlins and Dylan connected. Again, the Australian's indefatigable spirit led him to 'hang out' with Dylan. With the singer and his guitarist, Robbie Robertson, in tow, Rawlins conducted a 'tour' of Melbourne's Fitzroy district, at the time an underdeveloped area of the inner Melbourne that housed many of the city's poor in low rent, dilapidated housing (Hoskyns

2003: 115). It was one of the centres for the urban Indigenous community who were initally removed from cultural lands and then moved on again when Christian missions had closed (Australia's Indigenous people were not recognized as citizens to be counted in the national census until after 1968). Rawlins joined Dylan's tour entourage to Adelaide and in Sydney he took Dylan to the nearby Blue Mountains apparently to take acid. Thus, Rawlins cemented his place as a music insider whose opinions were to be respected. He would become one of Dylan's most ardent supporters in Australia, completing a book of essays about the singer, *Dylan through the Looking Glass: A Collection of Writings on Bob Dylan* (Rawlins 1994).

During the Dylan tour Rawlins experienced an epiphany, that music was a spiritual vehicle, and this stopped him in his tracks. After this experience Rawlins found himself unable to engage meaningfully with writing. He dropped out of working for *Music Maker* and other publications. Reflecting some years later he 'underwent many psychic and spiritual changes and was pretty well wiped out so that I became a sort of recluse' (Letter to Gavin [*sic*] Disney, 1972). Around the middle of 1968 he reappeared in Sydney working with musician and visual artist Lindsay Bourke, who had two years earlier staged the first mixed media show in Sydney's Cell Block Theatre. Rawlins penned his first *Music Maker* review for several years writing about an esoteric blues man, Wally Mudd (aka Warwick Wyld) and his band the Starving Wild Dogs, that played around Taylor Square in Darlinghurst. But it was Rawlins's encounter with the La De Da's in their psychedelic phase that brought him back to pop music. He told Gavan Disney, general manager of *Go Set*, that 'I heard the La De Das and recognised a real musical greatness in what they were doing'.

Despite his low-key public profile, Rawlins continued to work his contacts. He moved to Sydney and picked up occasional work with Clifford Hocking, who had himself moved on from selling records to managing an international touring company. Rawlins wrote press releases and other publicity pieces for Hocking's company while maintaining himself in low rent accommodation. During this period of intense of introspection, Rawlins continued to wander between cities and into the hippie communities that were emerging in the warmer climes, north of Sydney, and he maintained a network of contacts and couches across the east coast of Australia. By the time Rawlins met members of the La De Da's around October 1968, he had lost none of his stature as a recognized figure in Australia's counter-culture. Kevin Borich recalls Rawlins and his impact on the La De Da's:

> Adrian was a bit of a hero to us because he had interviewed Bob Dylan, and that was very impressive to us. He had this thing that he would, he would sort of over laugh, you know. He was […] that sort of personality that was just kind of full of joy. Sometimes people just thought he was nuts. We put up with it because he was creative.

This observation was shared by Juno Gemes, who had established the 10 Cunningham Street performance space in Sydney that also involved Rawlins. She said Rawlins 'loved music and musicians as a medium for the Divine, in a Sufic sense. He was a great catalyst who encouraged the creativity of others' (McIntyre 2006: 120). Encouragement for creativity was not the only thing that Rawlins offered to the band. With regard to acid rock direction that the La De Da's began to move in following their first visit to Sydney Rawlins provided an important link to the scene. Sydney was city of sandstone and beaches. The surf community provided an audience and site for the new youth focussed creativity that undergirded the shift from beat music to psychedelia. In the 1960s, innovative young filmmakers were producing their own surf movies and distributing them through schools and surf clubs. They brought in bands such as Taman Shud to provide soundtracks. As Ian McFarlane (2017) explains in the liner notes for the Shud's psychedelic release *Evolution* (1969), 'local surfing culture … was based around freedom of expression, expanded consciousness and getting back to nature' (see also Thoms 2000). The surfing community became an important audience for emerging psychedelia. While the La De Da's were welcomed in Sydney's surfside suburbs like Cronulla, coming from Auckland they did not have the deep links to this audience like other Sydney bands. Rawlins provided alternative pathways into the emerging acid rock and psychedelic communities that were connected to theatre and arts.

In September 1967, the La De Da's returned to New Zealand. Soon after Brett Nielsen called it a day with the band. While they picked up a new drummer, they also recharged their coffers. Despite nearly six months leave, the band had lost none of their pulling power in New Zealand. Chart success eluded them in Sydney and Melbourne but in Auckland they had two top ten hits. On their return they steered clear of Eldred Stebbing's Galaxie instead securing a residency at the Radio Hauraki supported venue, 1480 Village. But the band still had a desire to play in larger markets and to find a studio with expertise to support their aspirations for *The Happy Prince*. They settled into preparing themselves for their next tilt at success in Australia.

4   'Come And Fly With Me'

Return and renewal

The La De Da's second visit to Sydney began in February 1968. Coincidentally, the plane they were on also carried Dinah Lee's manager Jim Haddleton. He informed the band that, now that Lee was moving to the England, Bobi Nicholas had taken up a job in a newly formed booking agency, Cordon Bleu (Petch). The band had always maintained a wary distance from managers, preferring their own counsel and independence, but their initial Sydney experience demonstrated the importance of a booking agency in both Sydney and Melbourne to arrange gigs and media appearances. They decided to look in on Bobi at the new agency. The relationship they developed with Cordon Bleu would prove to be one of the most important in the band's career.

The La De Da's were returning to Sydney without Brett Nielsen, their drummer of the last four years. He was burnt by his prior experience in Australia and had decided to move in new musical direction: 'I also wondered where the La De Da's were going, maybe they … needed a different type of drummer. La De Da's music wasn't static it was always moving. It was always full of ideas' (Nielsen). The new sticks man was not of the band's choosing. He had arrived at the instigation of Nielsen, who, impressed with the sophisticated soul music of Auckland band, The Action, arranged to swap places with that band's drummer, Bryan Harris. Within six months Harris had also moved on after his band members decided they wanted to change drummers.

The band arrived with renewed commitment to record *The Happy Prince*. At least one track, 'Come and Fly with Me', had made it into their performance repertoire but they needed enough original songs to make up an album (see also Jenkins 2023). The band understood that the project put them at the edge of where music was going. Following the release of The Beatles' *Sgt. Pepper's Lonely Hearts Club Band* the field was wide open for what an album might be. With the changing conceptions of musical structures and the success of album sales, songs themselves were challenging radio play-imposed durations. The band were listening to Traffic, Vanilla Fudge, Jimi Hendrix and The Band, one time backing musicians of Bob Dylan, all of whom were innovating with song forms. *The Happy Prince* had become more significant than simply a structure for thinking through song writing: it would be a statement about where the band was with regard to international pop music. Late in 1967 the Fifth Dimension had released *The Magic Garden*, a song cycle largely written by Jimmy Webb that reflected a doomed love affair. There were stories emerging in early 1968 that The Who and the Small Faces, both of whom participated in a raucous tour of Australian and Aotearoa/New Zealand in January 1968, were working on elaborate rock operas (*Ogdens' Nut Gone Flake* was released by the Small Faces on 24 May 1968 with side two featuring an original fable about 'Happiness Stan'. The Who's *Tommy*, crediting Meher Baba as avatar, came out in 1969). The Pretty Things, who had made such an impact when they toured New Zealand in 1966 that they were barred from the country, brought out *S.F. Sorrow* in November 1968, just as the La De Da's were preparing to finally record their own artistic statement. Closer to home, a Melbourne-based band from Adelaide, the Twilights, had leveraged an unsuccessful television series pilot into a loosely connected story album called *Once upon a Twilight* … (June 1968) (Ian McFarlane 1999: 653). When it was released in 1969, *The Happy Prince* had a stronger social conscience than these projects, bar possibly *Tommy*, which came out after the La De Da's record. The La De Da's songs hit out at social hypocrisy and the self-interest and corruption of public officials and exemplified Wilde's message of redemption through 'a good act'.

The Happy Prince as it was being conceived was a parable of redemption and a tragedy of obligation. The album was produced as an interpretation of literature and followed the narrative set out by Wilde in his fable with specific songs accentuating the characters and action. In engaging with literature specifically the La De Da's project would break new ground in contemporary music. While literature had been an influence in popular music (Boyd 2023), the adaption of a complete story into the pop-rock idiom was a bold move. Literature had already inspired titles such as the Velvet Underground's 'Venus in Furs' (1966) and Cream's 'Tales of Brave Ulysses' (1967). In particular, Grace Slick's 'White Rabbit' (1967), performed with Jefferson Airplane, highlighted a psychotropic interpretation of Lewis Carrol's *Alice in Wonderland*. Deep Purple's second studio album, *The Book of Taliesyn* (1968), drew from the ancient Welsh book of poetry of that name but only one song, 'Listen, Learn, Read On', contains a lyrical reference to the book. In its conception, *The Happy Prince* was bolder and more ambitious than these songs and albums. When it was produced in early 1969 the album proved to be a novel engagement of literature and song in storytelling. It is not clear if the idea of including a narrator was related to the Small Faces' approach to storytelling but it did assist in maintaining fidelity to the original text, possibly a testament to the impact of the Welles and Crosby recording on band members. While 1968 would prove to be the year when the band finally secured what they needed to record their project, there were disappointments ahead for the group as they attempted to find both a studio, and a producer that would support their ambitions.

Cordon Bleu

While the band struggled to find a suitable place to record, they developed a stable and productive partnership for performance with Harry Widmer's Cordon Bleu, where they signed on soon after arriving back in Australia. In establishing his agency Widmer had said: 'Pop is a big business, … but it's so badly organised and the performers don't get a fair go. It's time someone stepped in and tried to run it like any other efficient business' (*Sun Herald* 1968a: 89). Widmer was an innovator who initially took to band management in 1966 on a whim and a dare (he bet a colleague he could successfully market an unknown product and chose a band, The Associates, who became The Executives). Queensland born but educated in Zurich, Widmer was living in Switzerland until he was twenty. He returned to Australia and in 1961 became the director of industrial design at the electronics company Kriesler, a division of the massive Dutch Philips group. He received numerous design awards including, in 1966, one for designing the Kreisler Mini 41–47 radio with polypropylene case, the first such application of the plastic anywhere in the world. He continued with Phillips while managing The Executives (Jones 2015: 16) and establishing Cordon Bleu in 1968. He had a vision for his music management company to become a full-service agency. Cordon Bleu's original bands – which included The Executives, and Max Merritt and the Meteors among others – were offered a wage with agency benefits including personal management and assistance with publicity, accounting and medical care (*Sun-Herald* 1968a). Writing in *Billboard* (1968: 45), *Sun-Herald* columnist Jock Veitch (who had the annoying custom of misspelling the band as the La-De-Dahs) reported that bands managed by Widmer will share profits from dances that he ran and that 'he had hired a business survey team to find the most populated teenage and young adult areas' to target for expansion. Not all Widmer's exploits were successful. His attempt to cash in on the city's discotheque boom, by turning a Chinese restaurant into a venue called Momma Monkey and Child, failed. Cordon Bleu managed Sydney gigs for its clients, but a separate agency was required for work in Melbourne, where the Michael Browning Entertainment Agency had exclusive booking for the La De Da's. Browning and Widmer were loosely associated under the banner of the Australian Entertainment Exchange (AEE). Browning had personal links with the owners of Sebastian's and Berties discotheques in Melbourne and so was able to secure gigs in the major Melbourne venues.[1]

Cordon Bleu set up offices in a cheap, inner-city area on Sussex Street, an undesirable street on the western fringe of the Sydney CBD. Jim Towers, whom Harry had plucked from the Wayside Chapel's Teenage Cabaret to help him book bands, recalled musicians traipsing up the steps to pick up the regular 'wage' from the agency (Towers). The area had been earmarked for a new freeway flyover – The Western

Distributor – that took much longer to construct than had been anticipated. First mooted in the late 1950s but operational only in the early 1970s, the road consisted of a double viaduct and a series of ramps creating various entry and departure points for the city. Once it was connected to the Kings Cross tunnel the Western Distributor provided through traffic flows from west to east, relieving the congested, bloated heart of the city – the central business district. The agency worked out of what was the city's oldest remaining market building known as the Corn Exchange. Constructed in 1887 with a curved wall and faux ionic columns built into the façade, the building had lost its former glory and was an informal homeless shelter through much of the 1960s. In 1964, the Sydney City Council funded an innovative theatre cooperative PACT (Producers, Authors, Composers and Talent) to set up in the Corn Exchange. When Cordon Bleu arrived PACT already had a performance space and a partly soundproof rehearsal room that the agency's bands could use. Harry Widmer eventually became the chairman of PACT's board. Later Essex, a music rights and publishing company also moved in and Essex signed the La De Da's Trevor Wilson and Bruce Howard to a publishing deal immediately before the pair went into the studio to record *The Happy Prince*. While Cordon Bleu slummed it for office rentals, Widmer chose the Here disco, across the Bridge in fashionable North Sydney for weekly Tuesday showcases for industry insiders, with acts which were booked by Bobi Nicholas (See Figure 4.1). These performances were an important introduction to the Sydney media and music community (Towers). The Here became a crucial meeting place in Sydney's pop music scene, all the more important because it was out of the whirl of the city's CBD.

The old Corn Exchange's cheap rental, due to its precarious positioning, may well have contributed to the incredible

Figure 4.1 *Bobi Nicholas at the Here disco with the La De Da's Kevin Borich in the background. Bobi Petch Collection.*

productivity that emerged from the site. As a performance space PACT drew in a diverse range of traditional and experimental artists. Margret RoadKnight made her first recording at PACT's regular folk music event. Impresario Jim Sharman began his career with 'On-stage Oz', a cabaret drawn from the pages of *Oz* magazine, and Graham Bond (who became television cult figure Aunty Jack in the 1970s) set up his performance nights at PACT. Poetry was staged with lightshows, rock bands and performers. In 1967, Australia's first experimental theatre group, The Human Body, was formed and began their performances – ceremonies – at PACT Theatre in 1968 (Gorman 2010). The Human Body had been established by Clem Gorman, Johnny Allen and Juno Gemes, who also set up 10 Cunningham St, the performance space behind Chequers nightclub. This was the Sydney scene that attracted Adrian Rawlins.

It's not clear where the La De Da's members actually met Rawlins. It may have been on the steps of the old Corn Exchange, although in truth it could have been anywhere in Sydney. Emerging from his period of intense introspection after his encounter with Dylan, Adrian Rawlins became ubiquitous. He could be found at EMI's Record Division offices in Castlereagh Street cadging records for review. Apparently, he was good friends with EMI's popular engineer-producer David Woodley-Page (Weule), who would go on to produce *The Happy Prince* when the band finally secured studio time for the album at EMI. Rawlins was regularly seen around the Cross as well, often distributing the psychedelically informed newspaper 'Chaos' on behalf of its publisher, poet and occult mystic Nevill Drury (*Shadowplay*). The band members may have attended one of Rawlins's own performances such as when he recited 'Howl' semi-naked at Sydney University's Refectory. Or Rawlins may have simply turned up to one of their gigs and inveigled his way back stage waving one or another press card. As Kevin Borich said when I asked when was Rawlins engaged to be the narrator of their album: 'He was already there.' Rawlins himself notes that he was invited by the band to sit in on rehearsals for recording *The Happy Prince* in November 1968. The recording sessions fell through and, by this failure, earn their place among the mythic stories of what I have dubbed 'the lost sessions'.

The lost sessions

The lost sessions are one of the intriguing and enduring mysteries of the La De Da's attempts to record *The Happy Prince*. There have been various descriptions of these sessions, which are deemed to have occurred sometime in 1968 but seem to be confused with the disastrous 1967 session for Sunshine at Festival's dilapidated Harris St studio. It is important to address discrepancies between these versions and to set the record straight because what is clear is that it was this confluence of circumstances which brought the band and Rawlins together to materialize a final shape for the elusive record. When all other avenues were shut off, the EMI sessions were a last-ditch effort by the band to successfully record in Australia.

One version of the lost sessions of 1968 has the band booked into record at Bill Armstrong's studios when the label they had lined up, Sweet Peach, pulled out after the band had spent three weeks rehearsing (Dix 1988: 71). Another version has the band recording the complete album in demo form before Sweet Peach pulled out and, further, the friction of the failed sessions led to drummer Bryan Harris being booted out (*The Happy Prince* 2005).[2] A final version again using the same source – the band's former drummer Bryan Harris – states that the sessions were in Sydney for the Sunshine label, who wiped the tapes after the band walked out (Gillanders & Welsh: 168–9). These attempts to piece together the story of the lost sessions are all occurring well after the events. Dix's book was closest to the time but still published fourteen years after the sessions were supposed to have taken place. The remastered CD liner notes – which were written by Grant Gillanders – are more than thirty years after the sessions and the final version, a retake of the liner notes with the Sunshine label inserted instead of Sweet Peach, is fifty years past the event. They could simply be understood and set aside as the inevitable vagaries of memory, recollections that have become indistinct with the fog time. However, some five decades plus on from the events, these circumstances are important. The lost sessions, and the subsequent frustration of the La De Da's not finding adequate recording arrangements in Australia, were the catalyst for Rawlins's enthusiastic encouragement for the band to stitch up a deal to access the EMI's Sydney 301 studios, where recording finally took place, early in 1969.

We can at least determine that that much is correct. Rawlins detailed the events leading up to the EMI studio recording in an article for *The Age* (Rawlins 1969). He wrote that, prior to finalizing the album recording at EMI in Sydney, there had been sessions scheduled for Adelaide in October 1968 and that, given the group were 'still smarting from disappointment at the cancellation [of those sessions] … it seemed that would be the last we would hear of *The Happy Prince*' (ibid). Rawlins wrote that he met the band again in December 1968 when he saw them perform at the Here discotheque in North Sydney. At this point he urged them to continue with the project. With Bruce Howard taking the initiative and Cordon Bleu stumping up the money for the studio hire, a publishing deal was finalized with Essex and the EMI recording sessions for the album were initiated.

Meanwhile, there are inconsistencies in the accounts that rely on Bryan Harris. Harris stated for 2005 remaster liner notes and, later, in Gillanders & Welsh (2019: 166) that he attended a recording session with the band but, between the accounts, the label changes – the 2005 liner notes refer to Sweet Peach yet Gillanders and Walsh's later account in 2019 has the sessions at Sunshine in Sydney. This revised account needs further investigation. Sessions for the Sunshine label, so early on the band's return are unlikely given the poor relationship that developed when they were in the studios with that label's producer, Steve Neale, in 1967. It is possible that, after they returned to Australia in 1968, the band did record for Festival who had been distributing Sunshine. There is a report that the La De Da's had signed with Festival soon after they arrived back in Australia in May 1968 (*Sun Herald* 1968b: 59) – but there is no mention of any recording sessions. When I talked with Bryan Harris, he insisted that there had been a recording session while he was in the band in Sydney. His description of 'a modern studio, sprung floor, near the Pyrmont Bridge' (Harris) coincides with the conditions and location of the new Festival studios on Pyrmont Road. Cordon Bleu had strong connections with Festival at this time. Jim Towers described a close working relationship between Pat Aulton (former Sunshine house producer, then working at Festival) and Tymepiece, a band managed by Cordon Bleu.[3] This relationship between the agency and the label makes it more likely that if, as Harris claims, the La De Da's went into a studio to record early on their return to Australia, it could have been for Festival. Still, these sessions remain a mystery. While the band was performing their new material, including 'Come And Fly With Me', which ended up on the album, there is no report of songs from *The Happy Prince* being recorded with Harris, other than his own anecdote.

The Sweet Peach label was most often associated by various sources with the La De Da's failed attempt to record the album. It featured in Harris's original story and it was referred to by John Dix, who claimed that Sweet Peach's sessions had been in Melbourne at Armstrong's studios, although again, there is no evidence that the Melbourne sessions ever occurred. In May 1968, just a few months before Harris left the band that label was little more than an aspiration. According to the respected pop journalist for the *Sydney Morning Herald* Michael Symons (1969a):

The label was launched on May 7, by talented British record producer and songwriter Jimmy Stewart and the equally young Adelaide man, the talented publicity designer Denis Whitburn. They had met a year earlier when Stewart was producing the successful single, 'The Love Machine' and Whitburn was editing a pop trade magazine *Immediate*.

(9)

Harris did not play with the band after September 1968, and it is highly unlikely that he and the band would have recorded anything in Sydney for Sweet Peach in May that year, given the very early stage of the label's formation. In any case Sweet Peach had strong connections with Adelaide and Gamba Studios, where Rawlins said the sessions had been scheduled.

The new drummer for the La De Da's – and the one that they recorded *The Happy Prince* with – was Keith Barber. Another expatriate Brit, Barber was with The Wild Cherries, who had once been the house band in Adrian Rawlins's old haunt, The Fat Black Pussycat in Toorak, Melbourne. Barber took his place with the La De Da's in September 1968 and later recalled being recruited for the band. While playing for The Wild Cherries, Barber remembered being on a tour to Sydney with the La De Da's and Max Merritt & the Meteors:

I ended up in the audience with a guy called John 'Yuk' Harrison, who was the bass player in Max Merritt's band. We were sitting there watching the La De Da's and he said, 'what do you think' and I said, 'I reckon they're great'. He nudged me in the side and said, 'you could be playing drums with that band if you want to'. I didn't think anything more of it, but went back to the hotel where all the bands were staying in King's Cross. One morning the La De Da's walked in minus their drummer and asked me if I'd like to join. I had a sense that the Cherries were fragmenting and that I wasn't going to cause the split by leaving … I really admired the La De Da's, so I accepted the offer.

(Warburton 2009)

With Barber in the band the group began to consolidate its psychedelic sound.

Jim Stewart, the founder of Sweet Peach, is an important cog in this (rumour) mill. Stewart was an expatriate Irishman who found his way into Australian pop in the mid 1960s. His production on 'The Love Machine' for Pastoral Symphony, an early studio 'super group', created a psychedelic gem that was a hit in Melbourne and other cities in May 1968. Pastoral Symphony was a confected band made up largely of the Twilights, along with a couple of other vocalists (*Milesago* 'Groups and solo artists: Pastoral Symphony').[4] The sound that Stewart created was enhanced by Armstrong's engineer Roger Savage, who produced a phasing effect by running two playback machines slightly out of sync (Stewart). Stewart also used strings and heavy reverberation on the voices that may well have been attractive to the La De Da's, who were looking for a studio and an ambitious producer that could accommodate their ideas for *The Happy Prince*. Stewart was a man driven by ambitions, and even though Sweet Peach would not be launched for another year or so, he was looking out for projects. For production facilities Stewart had developed a link in Adelaide with Gamba Studios which was supported by the deep pockets of Derek Jolly, heir to a fortune generated by winemakers, Penfolds. Gamba Studios was a state-of-the-art recording studio kitted out with the highest-quality recording equipment available. Derek Jolly encouraged an open-door policy, inviting musicians and performers to use the studios to experiment with their music. At this stage, in late 1968, Jolly was negotiating to secure a Moog synthesizer for his studios, one of the few of these instruments available outside of the United States. This was the destination that the La De Da's were enroute to when they were informed the session would not take place.[5]

These sessions at Gamba were genuinely lost. There are numerous contemporaneous reports that point to a relationship between Sweet Peach, Gamba and the La De Da's. In October 1968, Sydney's *Sun-Herald* reported the band were busy 'writing a new L.P. called *The Happy Prince* which they will play at Derek Jolly's Adelaide studios for Sweet Peach Productions in four weeks' (*Sun Herald* 1968c: 103). Exactly four weeks later, though, *Go Set* broke the news that the sessions had been the cancelled:

> On Tuesday night the La De Da's were all set to go to Adelaide to record their third album, *The Happy Prince*. They had packed their bags, loaded the vans and were ready to go … [T]hey decided to ring Adelaide and confirm the recording studio address. But they were told the studios weren't even completed and that the session was off.
>
> (*Go Set* 1968: 7)

Other contemporaneous reports claimed that the studio had either been demolished ('It's been a nightmare') or destroyed by fire, despite there being no verifiable reports that there was any damage to the Gamba Studios. The band took some of the time they had set aside for Adelaide to retreat to regional Victoria for creative work, during which time they worked out nine songs (Rawlins 1969). Rawlins downplayed the disappointment of the La De Da's at losing another opportunity to record their LP. The band had not managed to record any music since their initial foray to Australia nearly eighteen months earlier. For musicians who were proficient in the studio as a creative space, this would have been frustrating, let alone the difficulty created by not having an album to tour and sell. The band revealed that they had decided not to record in Australia and would go to England to cut a new record (*Go Set* 1968: 7). This was the position that Rawlins found them in when he caught up with them in Sydney some weeks later where he encouraged them to think again about recording the album locally.

Disco gods

The band's disenchantment with recording in Australia came at a time when their East Coast profile was at an all-time high. The band was based in Sydney, but with the support of Cordon Bleu in Sydney and Michael Browning's agency in Melbourne, they had ensured they were performing at the right places in Australia's biggest cities. While they had received a bad rap from a key Melbourne DJ in 1967 – Stan Rofe had opined in his column in *Go Set* that he was 'not impressed with the La De Das' (Rofe 1967: 3) – they had garnered strong support from another of the important pop journalist in that city, Ian 'Molly' Meldrum.

Meldrum showed up at *Go Set* soon after it started publication in 1966. Founder and then university drop-out Philip Frazer later quipped: 'He knew a lot more about venues and bands than we did so I figured we should work with him' (McIntyre 2006: 25). Meldrum cultivated the scene in Melbourne, turning up at parties, gigs, studios, anywhere that he could connect with pop music. He managed Russell Morris both in his initial band Somebody's Image and later when he undertook a successful solo career. From 1965, Meldrum worked as a mime performer in Melbourne's jukebox tv show *Kommotion*, an arrangement that ended disastrously when most of the show's performers, including Meldrum, left due to a dispute with the producers. *Kommotion* limped on but Actors Equity placed bans on the programme due to concerns over employment for musicians given the songs were recordings. Soon after, Meldrum added the role of columnist to his duties as a feature writer for *Go Set*, beginning the regular 'Keyholes' column where he would often name drop the La De Da's, thus becoming an important conduit between the band and readers of *Go Set*.

The band had adapted their performance style to the discotheque scene they experienced in Australia. A discotheque's atmosphere was built around constant music providing the most opportunity for dancing. DJ sets would blend into band performances, allowing for a seamless experience of various kinds of music. The La De Da's adopted this style to their own sets. Writing in *Go Set* late in 1968 Meldrum described their music, promoting the idea that 'many people look upon the band as "Gods" of the disco scene' (Meldrum 1968: 7).[6] In a gushing style that became typical of Meldrum – especially during his thirteen years (1974 to 1987) as host of Australia's hit TV pop show *Countdown* – he wrote:

> Everything about the La De Das is exceptional. They have a great understanding in their music because they have a great understanding among themselves. One number they perform on stage relies on a complete understanding between musicians and singer alike. The number is titled 'Yesterday, Today, Tomorrow' and if the understanding is there, the song can last for well over thirty minutes.
>
> (ibid)

As musicians Meldrum said they were 'pioneers' who loved to experiment with new instruments and new sounds. Rawlins had a more grandiose, but nonetheless interesting, take on the music the La De Da's had adopted at this point. Using the example of Dvořák, he compared their work to European romantic programme music whereby a specific narrative is developed to evoke extra-musical ideas or images in the listener (Rawlins 1969). This is likely the source of the references whereby the band's music was compared to the composer or, as Dix claims, that they used Dvořák's work in their performances (Dix 1988: 71). Throughout 1968, with the steady income from Cordon Bleu's innovative arrangement with their bands, the La De Da's members expanded their equipment. John Dix (1988) wrote that they backed their ambitious experiments with a big sound: 'As their popularity increased so did their finances, which they poured back into their music. By the end of 1968, the La De Da's instrumentation included Hammond organ, Fender Rhodes piano, saxophones, flute, sitar, bagpipes, mandolin and cello' (70). The extended performance sets also reflected the often acid-fuelled improvisation sessions that passed as rehearsals. The discotheque as a performance stage assisted the band in developing extended jamming and improvisation that fitted the psychedelic persona they had adopted for Australia's east coast. In December 1968, *Go Set*'s readers voted the band the best Australian disco act.

5 *The Happy Prince*

The EMI sessions

David Woodley-Page came to EMI in 1967 after beginning his career as a recording studio technician and engineer at Amalgamated Wireless Australia (AWA) in Sydney. Eventually he became the trusted name of high-end hi-fi for the home, spruiking turntables in full-page ads for new audio consumers (*Sydney Morning Herald* 1976: 9; *Sydney Morning Herald* 1980: 16). David's father died when he was twelve years old. He grew up in Waverton, an inner Northern suburb on the harbour, with both his mother and his sister Jillian. David threw himself into the emerging electrical sound technology and converted his bedroom to an audio engineering lab (Porteous). He was also an accomplished musician who studied under Norman Johnston, an esteemed organist and pianist, at St Peter's Church in East Sydney (Bakker). Woodley-Page performed in piano recitals broadcast for the Australian Broadcasting Commission in the early 1960s and was part of a singing group with Jillian, Brian Buggy (a classical musician and conductor) and David Mackay, who recalled: 'We had a group called The Unknowns … because we were unknown. It was just good fun. We got together to record sort of good things, but they weren't commercial' (Mackay). With a background in music and electronics, aware of the most recent developments in studio production, Woodley-Page became a trusted collaborator in the studio when he worked with the La De Da's to record *The Happy Prince.* His appreciation of importance of keyboards would have helped him build a rapport with Bruce Howard, who had become more assertive with regard to the band's directions as he developed into the group's most capable songwriter. Rawlins recalls Woodley-Page as 'a very imaginative producer … who knew music and could communicate apparently most effectively with Bruce' (1969). But Woodley-Page and the band would have to deal with the recording environment established in Sydney by EMI – then one of the largest recording and whitegoods conglomerates in the world.

Mackay had become friends with Woodley-Page after meeting him at AWA. Mackay was a panel operator at Radio 2CH, the radio station AWA owned while Woodley-Page was a studio engineer. Mackay made the move to EMI's recording studios in 1965, and a couple of years later Woodley-Page followed him there. The recording studios were just one part of EMI activities at 301 Castlereagh Street. In residence at the address since the late 1950s, the international conglomerate took up all nine floors. On the ground floor was its whitegoods showroom, which was followed by four floors for sales and servicing. The Records Division was on fifth floor. EMI had three studios on the eighth floor with the cutting rooms above that on the ninth. With EMI's enormous resources, Studio 301, as the main studio became known, was at one time the most advanced in Australia, having the first fully transistorized mixing console designed and built by EMI, installed in 1962 and introducing Scully four-track half-inch machines for music recording in 1965. Still, the Australian arm was slow to keep pace with the rapidly changing field of popular music recording, especially compared to more nimble independent studios such as Bill Armstrong's in Melbourne. In 1968, Armstrong installed one of the first eight-track recorders in the country. EMI did not update Studio 301 to eight-track recorders until a year later, which was too late for the La De Da's recording.

While Woodley-Page was still at AWA, Mackay began to make a name for himself at EMI as an engineer. When a producer left EMI at short notice, Mackay was asked to step in as an engineer/producer on a session for the Twilights, who, in 1966, were recording their fourth single, 'Bad Boy' (Mackay). The song was a success, leading Mackay to be recognized as a rising star in the company. Later that year he was appointed head of the Records Division's Artists and Repertoire (A&R). Mackay also became the Twilights' long-term recording collaborator, producing their album *Once upon a Twilight* … While pleased with the production result and the fact that the band came back to work with him again Mackay was nevertheless concerned about the culture at EMI when it came to recording pop music:

> They were very fuddy-duddy, you know. They were very nice men, but … they weren't into modern recording and [had not] tried to push the envelope … the studio existed more on doing orchestral things, TV, lots of commercials. So doing records was just a part of that. Most of their money would have come from the big orchestras that were doing jingles. EMI in those days sold televisions; they sold record players; they sold virtually everything. They weren't just a record company.[1]

When it came to recording the company had its own standards as to what was appropriate for cutting discs. Mackay soon decided, with the blessing of EMI, that he would take his recording work to Armstrong's in Melbourne:

> [I]f I mixed a record, I'd take it and they would, cut the masters up on the ninth floor. And, you know, we'd say, 'Oh,

come on, we need to get the level up on this. We need this to crunch you know, make this sound really strong'. But I found that I was getting far better results by having Bill Armstrong cut the masters himself in Melbourne. He was much more on our side … he would go the extra mile. Whereas at EMI: 'Oh no it needs to be this level, and it needs to be like that'. Bill Armstrong … supported us and gave us a chance to do what we wanted to do.

The studio itself also had limitations. Mackay called it 'antiseptic' while gun New Zealand producer, Howard Gable, who came to produce for EMI, refused to work there and based himself in Melbourne. He told the music television programme *Wrokdown* (2016): 'I went to Sydney first and hated Sydney. The studios there were like an old barn. It was more like a hospital than it was a rock and roll joint' (See Figure 5.1). Mackay tells a story that may be apocryphal: 'Wally, the chief engineer at EMI, had a buzzer … If the guys in the studio downstairs, were listening to the monitor too loud, a bell would go off, and he'd come down and take you off.'

When Woodley-Page came to EMI in 1967 Mackay had blazed a trail for the producer/engineer. By then he had come to the attention of the London office. Mackay was asked to produce and record at the Abbey Road Studios and was replaced by Howard Gable. Despite Mackay's success in using Armstrong's in Melbourne to master and mix EMI recordings, there was little likelihood that Woodley-Page would follow that path. In 1968, when he took on the sessions for the La De Da's in Studio 301 to record *The Happy Prince*, Woodley-Page and his wife of recent years Ursula were expecting their first child (Bakker). He was not about to be wandering back and forth between Sydney and Melbourne on a recording odyssey. In any case it is unlikely that the Records Division would have allowed it. At this time, late in 1968, they had a rogue amateur producer causing havoc in the Armstrong studios in EMI's name. Molly Meldrum had decided to add studio production to his list of experiences. He had taken the singer he managed, Russell Morris, into Armstrong's to record for EMI's Columbia label. He sabotaged the initial song choice, favoured by the label, so that Morris would have to record a song that Molly believed was right for his singer (Meldrum 2016: 123–4). This song became one of the longest singles ever released in the country and the chaotic sessions were some the most expensive that EMI had been involved with in Australia (Meldrum 2016: 125–8). Still, all was eventually forgiven as Meldrum had produced Russell Morris's psychedelic pop anthem 'The Real Thing', which reached No. 1 in Australia in May 1969.

Figure 5.1 *Kevin Borich l. and Bruce Howard r. at the recording of* The Happy Prince *in Studio 301 which one producer described as 'an old barn … more like a hospital than it was a rock'n'roll joint'. National Film and Sound Archive (Australia) Collection.*

In studio

These circumstances left the La De Da's to record in Sydney's 301 studio. The final result of album's recording is, in some ways, a testament to Mackay's assessment that the studio was antiseptic and the mastering process was conservative. The huge studio included orchestra chairs piled up along its walls. In the end there is a flatness to the sound of the album that gives it a distant, reserved feel. The situation may have been impacted by the fact, as I discussed earlier, that the band had almost given up on recording and had only just managed to stitch together the support they needed to get time in the studio: they certainly were not about to jeopardize this one last chance to record the album by suggesting the studio was not up to scratch, although later Borich would refuse to record in Studio 301 for a follow-up album for EMI. The benefit of the EMI studio facilities was that they afforded excellent professional resources for recording. Rawlins and Key made use of the smaller Studio C to record narration and lyrics, while featured tracks could be separated by recording in Studio B, with the whole band coming together in the large main studio, where they took the opportunity to engage the range of their musical skills.

Despite the constraints, the recording was a success. It demonstrated technical innovation and creative endeavour so that the sessions would produce one of the most critically acclaimed albums of Oceania in the 1960s. Woodley-Page certainly went as far as he could to develop the technical conditions that would allow the band to capture the big sound that they were working with. An opening pastoral instrumental tune on flute (by Kevin Borich) leads into Rawlins's initial narration where he describes the arrival of The Swallow to the shoulder of The Happy Prince. These two figures – The Prince and The Swallow – are the dual protagonists in the story. The Swallow interrupts his journey, following his flock south to the Nile for winter. He hears The Prince's tale, how he was once happy – 'if pleasure be happiness' – but is no longer. Now a statue, placed high above the city, he can see misery he had not previously encountered. The initial song of this side, 'Covered in Gold', sets out the condition of The Prince: covered in gold but no longer happy. From his vantage point he sees what 'happens on the other side of town'.[2] The track outlines the concern of the story: 'Unwanted people / so poor they're weak and starving / … Can't you see the problem'. Rawlins's narration sets out the first task for The Swallow: to remove the ruby from The Prince's sword hilt and take it to a mother and her ill son, who do not have the food they need. Initially protesting that he is waited for in Egypt, The Swallow agrees to stay one night to help The Prince as his messenger, thus sealing his fate. By the end of the story, having completed The Prince's requests to strip him of his treasures and distribute them across the city, The Swallow dies at the foot of the statue. The track 'Ruby for a Lady' showcases Phil Key's soulful voice, soaring over a rather ponderous tune from Howard's Hammond organ and flute from Borich. The story line develops the moral: 'take this stone [ruby] from me and leave it in her care'. Rawlins's narration reinforces the key theme of the Wilde story of a 'good action', whereby taking the ruby to a poor family allows The Swallow to feel the glow from his undertaking leading to The Swallow's dream of flying with The Prince. This segues into the single culled from the album, 'Come And Fly With Me', which had been part of the band's repertoire for almost two years before being recorded. The track features strong funky bass riffs by Wilson.

The subsequent tracks, interspersed with narration, take on different characterizations and registers according to their role in the story. For instance, 'Swallow, Little Swallow' (Side 1, track 4) is more rhythmic than melodic. The tune is made up of constrained notes within a limited repetitive scale. Reflecting tension and resolution, it has the moral instruction common to nursery rhymes. This track picks up the narrative of The Prince petitioning his accomplice to stay. The tune's bass line continues under Rawlins's narration, emphasizing the macabre turn in The Swallow's role where The Prince calls on him to pluck out an eye 'made of rare sapphires'. The Swallow protests but does what he is asked. Side one ends with a dramatic six-minute ballad of extended verses. A short chorus, that you can't take wealth with you into the afterlife, directs the listener towards the deaths that await the protagonists of the story. The song is one of two that have a dialogic commentary embedded within them, here about the nature of success. There is a final narration where The Prince implores The Swallow to continue his journey south, and then the side closes with a *sotto voce* coda asking the listener to 'turn the page' and so emphasizing how the La De Da's long player operates as an interpretation of literature.

The second side begins with a chromatic musical overture titled 'Life Is Leaving': top heavy, bassy piano and plaintive flute give way to a redemptive pop-rock tune which leads to a piano-bass cadenza. The song 'Tales of The Nile' engages Bruce Howard as singer with a tale-telling lyric that sits amidst a complicated rollick. Along with his keyboard duties Howard took on marshalling technical know-how in the studio. Rawlins coyly noted David Woodley-Page and Howard's ongoing production dialogue: 'an incomprehensible and cryptic exchange of verbal symbols mainly consisting of "highs",

"lows", "ups", "downs" and sundry other equally brief utterances'
(Rawlins 1969).

Following Howard's opening rollick (Track 1 Side 2), the narration relates how The Prince finally asks The Swallow to strip him of the gold leaf that covers him and distribute it throughout the city. This final act leaves The Prince dull and grey and introduces the coming winter. From this climactic point ('Winter Song' Track 2 Side 2), complete with storm effects and staccato guitar, the story's dénouement is within sight. The depths of Wilde's story are plumbed in the narration which recounts the success of The Prince's undertaking through The Swallow's eyes, while the bird is in his death throes. The following song, 'Lullaby', is introduced with a homology of death as 'the brother of sleep', playing with the dualism of *la petite mort*, that momentary lapse of consciousness that is also a point of physical ecstasy. The ethereal tones of Borich's sitar emphasize a shift to a world beyond reason. As the death of The Swallow and The Prince draws near, so does their redemption. Here, Rawlins narrates Wilde's most audacious contribution to the fairy tale genre: a kiss on the mouth between the two male protagonists, after which The Swallow falls down dead and The Prince's leaden heart breaks. At this point the La De Da's engage in their most overtly theatrical approach. Dialogue introduces three city politicians who determine to tear down the dull, grey Prince, with the dead bird at his feet and argue about who should replace him. The track 'Civic Pride' could well be an ironic commentary on Auckland or Sydney. The song works as a libretto whereby the city's politicians – Mayor, City Clerk and a 'man from the Ministry' – argue about which of them should be the next statue after they have torn down The Prince, only to be told by the people they want roads instead. The penultimate narration sees the redemption of The Swallow and The Prince. This is emphasized by an interlude of Borich's sitar, the phrasing of which reflects a Maori chant that wells up from underneath and is pushed on by a church organ. The broken leaden heart and the deceased bird are collected by an angel on command of God to find 'the two most precious things in the city'. The album is closed out by the Māori chant morphing into Hallelujah and a final coda of church organ.

The Happy Prince was recorded over four weeks early in 1969 and completed on February 25. Friends, including Bobi Nicholas, would drop in to offer encouragement and observe the sessions. With Rawlins, the band was in the studio four nights a week for three weeks, working from 5.00 or 6.00 pm until midnight (when a higher rate for producers kicked in) (Rawlins 1969). The final production and mastering occurred through February that year. While Scully half-inch four-track recorders were standard in Studio 301, Woodley-Page had developed a technical innovation that allowed him to synchronize between two machines to create an eight-track recording. This reduced the process of 'bouncing down' – dubbing a completed four-track recording onto one track of another tape – which, as author and historian Jaesen Jones has noted, 'demanded skill, care and the best equipment, otherwise the build-up of noise on the master tape would become unacceptable' (personal communication). In deploying this creative approach to recording, Woodley-Page produced *The Happy Prince* as Australia's first eight-track long play records.

In terms of musical creativity, the sessions saw band members engaging instruments outside their usual forte. While Kevin had been playing sitar as part of their performances, this was the first time he recorded with the instrument. He also took up flute which was featured on a number of tracks. Phil Key played conga, while Bruce added tenor sax – again a performance instrument for him – to his regular keyboard duties. On one track the band included a Chinese gong they had found in an adjacent studio (Elfick 1969: 10). *Go Set*'s Sydney editor David Elfick noted the music and the theme set the material at a higher creative level than had hitherto been seen in Australian pop: 'If you believe that pop music is the literature of today, then Phillip, Keith. Kevin, Trevor and Bruce have made something which has creative and lasting value. They are not merely recording music to earn a living' (Elfick 1969). Meldrum showed his support for the band with a two-part track-by-track description of the album soon after the final masters were completed, prior to album's release. He told *Go Set* readers: 'The production used on *The Happy Prince* is utterly brilliant. It captures everything the story, the music and the feeling. The outstanding playing of instruments by the La De Da's leaves nothing to be desired' (1969a). Meldrum quoted other musicians' responses to hearing early cuts of the album saying Russell Morris was 'utterly possessed' by one of the tracks and that Yuk Harrison (from Max Merritt and the Meteors) couldn't stop raving about it. Brian Cadd described it as 'a work of musical art', while Meldrum himself concluded that it was 'the BEST production ever to come out of Australia' (1969b). Outside the coterie of musical compadres, the reviews were not so effusive. *The Age's* reviewer argued: 'Universal love is one thing. Universal appeal is another. This rather buddistically-slanted [*sic*] piece left me wondering who the group hoped to woo. Perhaps this is not as important as being true to oneself', adding that he found Rawlins's grandiose comparisons of the band's music 'a little hard to swallow' (Forester 1969).[3]

The band themselves seemed relieved to have the monkey off their back. In June 1969, soon after the release, they were on a plane to London. It appears that they undertook a full live performance of the album, including Rawlins's narration, for the Sydney music industry (Weule; David Lillicot personal communication), but as one news item noted, in a thinly ironic dig: 'Biggest L.P. release of week is the La De Dahs' [*sic*] *The Happy Prince* … The boys are on their way to England now and won't be around for the fuss, but they've taken copies with them' (Veitch 1969: 77). There was some expectation that EMI in London would look favourably upon them and provide support for performing and distributing the album in England but, as many antipodean pop bands had found before them, the 'home' country was not interested in what they had to say. EMI were only prepared to let them record Beatles covers from the *Abbey Road* album that was due to be released. With no performances to push the album locally – and it was a challenging pop album to be sure – the Australian media lost their enthusiasm. The album sunk without a trace in both markets.

Significance

The Happy Prince may have simply been too ambitious for commercial success. While cultural recycling pervades the history of song making in general (Ingham 2017), the La De Da's album is one of the very few albums to attempt to render literature into contemporary pop-rock. In its artistic aspirations the album was of its time, with rehearsals for the Sydney debut of the pop rock musical *Hair* being held contemporaneously with *The Happy Prince* studio sessions (*Hair's* Australian debut was in June 1969). Adrian Rawlins was closely associated with the performers in *Hair* and especially the band backing the performances, Tully, many of whom were also followers of Meher Baba. Rawlins's own infatuation with the Beat poets and his early experimentation with jazz and poetry was also resonant with what the band attempted (see Figure 5.2. Rawlins immortalised in Melbourne). The La De Da's opus was more than a jazz riff on poetry however, and much closer to literature than to theatre.[4] In flagging the textual inspiration of the music, the band was ahead of more overt progressive rock adventures such as Rick Wakeman's *Journey to the Centre of the Earth* (1974). It is likely that this textual borrowing led to a mislabelling of *The Happy Prince* an example of 'prog rock'. Kevin Borich rejected the prog rock reference – 'I don't even know what that is' (Borich) – but the mislabelling has remained (see for example Caddick 2018).

On the decision to go to England and not tour the album in Australia, Phil Key later quipped ironically, 'That was very smart', adding that 'we had some money and we didn't care' (Matheson 1975).[5] With hindsight, *The Happy Prince* recording repeated the experience the band had with their initial self-penned release 'Don't You Stand in My Way' (see Chapter 2). That single was pushed ahead by the band despite Stebbing's dictate that they record another cover as a safer way to get a hit, confirming the rift between the band and its producers. Similarly, taking *The Happy Prince* to England to promote, rather than engage in the accepted practice of touring the album in Australia, was a headstrong approach, the band thumbing their nose at industry conventions. Independence was one of the band's qualities, but it also undermined their overall success. Valuing independence, and being suspicious of authorities, the band also did without managers. The closest they got to accepting oversight was with the paternal relations they developed between Hugh Lynn their New Zealand road manager and Cordon Bleu's Harry Widmer. While the band had secured their dream of recording their passion project, in leaving for England without a manager they put significant pressure on themselves. This was a band in a hurry.

In transferring a structured narrative story to song, the La De Da's undertook a unique transposition. *The Happy Prince* provides the fullest expression of the band's take on interpretation, the artistic ambitions of which they gambled would be best recognized in the more sophisticated markets of England. This was not the case. Some critics have blamed the narrative voice of Adrian Rawlins as a reason that the album was not well received popularly despite being lauded by critics on release. Rawlins's contribution however is crucial to the

Figure 5.2 *Happiness but, no gold here. A statue of Adrian Rawlins, erected in 1994 in Brunswick St, Fitzroy, Melbourne to commemorate his contribution to poetry and the arts. Unknown photographer.*

album as a unique pop-rock recording. Realized in a moment of serendipitous camaraderie between a garrulous hippie and band of musical brothers, during an era when drugs were integral to accessing altered states so as to see the world anew, when art and pop intermingled in swirling city scenes whose reputations were not yet written, *The Happy Prince* remains a testament to pioneering New Zealanders and Australians – the musicians and their cohorts – who forged new approaches to music and performance in the antipodes.

6 Afterlife

At the beginning of the New Year, 1969, Ian 'Molly' Meldrum gave a 'crystal ball' forecast of the La De Da's prospects:

> [O]riginality will force them to head overseas. It will take them at least six months of hard saving before they can undertake this venture. During this six months they will record their long-awaited album, titled *The Happy Prince*. This will receive world-wide recognition, and London music publishers will be fighting to sign them up. The five wandering minstrels will refuse all offers and tour Europe gaining the necessary experience. By the end of this year, you can forget the Cream, Traffic and Hendrix because La De Das will be the thing.
>
> (*Go Set* 1969)

While wishful thinking underlies these speculations, they demonstrate two things: the high regard that the band had garnered over the course of 1968 when they returned to take on the Australian scene and, secondly, the critical place of *The Happy Prince* album in the band's career. In terms of the band, there was *before The Happy Prince* and *after The Happy Prince*. That album changed everything, but not in the way the band and their supporters expected.

The La De Da's had grown as musicians by investing in their music, learning how to play different instruments and opening up to new listening encounters. They embraced the discotheque as a venue to programme music in a style that had not been experienced in Australia previously. Long, uninterrupted sets that fed into a psychedelic-inspired encounter between mind and body in a dance environment, that in its own way predicted electronic dance music, more than prog-rock. But success was not born from musicality, which was the band's strong suit rather than the faux-originality touted by Meldrum. London music publishers were not interested when the band arrived at the beginning of the northern summer in 1969. Their belatedness was obvious. Led Zeppelin was reshaping contemporary rock music, moving away from short duration singles to long, extended album tracks while eschewing media for mystique and constant touring. Initially as the New Yardbirds, then as Led Zeppelin, the band had been on the road constantly since forming in late 1968, stopping long enough to go into Olympic Studios in London to record their eponymous debut LP. Writing in *Oz*, Felix Dennis called it 'a turning point in rock music' (1969). With this album, a mix of reworked covers and original material, Page emerged as a musician with a strong interest in creating distinctive moods in the band's recording and a unique live sound based around extended improvisations – the kind of style that the La De Da's were working with in their disco performances. Under Page, however, Led Zeppelin had initiated a new rock sound that at the same time realized some of the grander visions of what contemporary rock music could be. Along with bands such as King Crimson, whom the La De Da's went to see in London, the music scene was just so much more sophisticated than the band had experienced in Australia. While they arrived with *The Happy Prince* in hand, hoping that it would lead to further opportunities for creative work, they found their brand of interpretive rock was already superseded. This belatedness, along with the decision to leave Australia and New Zealand without touring the new album, led to the disappearance of *The Happy Prince*. The album, hailed as a ground-breaking production in Australia, remained unheard in Britain and Europe.

The dream that a place in the international music firmament existed for the La De Da's was finally abandoned. It proved to be nothing more than apophenia: faces in clouds come to take them far away from home, to paraphrase compatriot Bic Runga. A gambler's fallacy, that by rolling the dice and arriving in London with an album under their arms would open doors, only took them down a dark corridor. Six months later, without success in England, the band – minus bassist Trevor Wilson – returned to Australia.

The La De Da's had arrived in England with few contacts and no manager or equipment. At this time, Led Zeppelin had returned from their triumphant second tour of America and had taken a two-week break, their first time off since the band were formed. There were strong connections between Jimmy Page and New Zealand. He had toured there with the Yardbirds in the early 1968, immediately after Peter Grant had taken the reins as manager. Grant – who would also manage Led Zepplelin – remodelled the band's finances for that tour and it became the first time the musicians saw income directly from their performances (Organ 2015). Further, Clive Coulson – whose band The Mods had supported the Yardbirds in New Zealand – was now Led Zeppelin's road manager. Through one or another connection, the La De Da's found themselves hiring equipment for gigs from Led Zeppelin. Keith Barber recalled that it was not a productive relationship from his point of view: 'We got involved with Peter Grant … but he was just ripping us off … He was taking Led Zeppelin's equipment that was warehoused and making out that he was helping us out but in fact the La De Das were paying through the teeth for this equipment' (Warburton). The band attempted to interest Grant in *The Happy Prince*. They arranged to perform songs from the album for Grant and travelled up the M1 to meet the kingpin manager, but disaster struck. Borich recalls: 'Our van broke down. We were almost there. We were going to have a talk about it with him … Bruce and Trevor were going to pitch this story [of "The Happy Prince"] because it needs to have a big [sound] like that, because it was a musical' [Borich]. The plan was abandoned, and with Led Zeppelin and Grant touring soon after, the opportunity never came around again.

The band were reduced to following the whims of their production company, EMI where they were still under contract. And in England EMI's focus remained on The Beatles. With the *Abbey Road* album about to drop EMI offered the La De Da's an 'opportunity' to cover a track. They recorded 'Come Together' (as The La De Dah Band – it seems that their record label, now the EMI subsidary Parlaphone, couldn't even be bothered to spell their name correctly). Barber told Nick Warburton:

> We were given all of the *Abbey Road* songs before they were released and told that we could record one of these songs. We listened to the whole album and the only thing we could see the way clear to making a decent single out of was 'Come Together'. We recorded at Abbey Road and then went on a tour of France.

The band toured small venues in Europe, at one point crossing paths with Gene Vincent, who was on a comeback tour and joined them on stage. The success they craved eluded them and their single was scuttled when The Beatles also chose 'Come Together' along with 'Something' as a double A-side single release from *Abbey Road*. The next winter, in February 1970, the band returned to Australia. Trevor Wilson had decided to make the most of his British heritage and remained in London to try to make it there. On arriving back in Australia, the band recruited a new bass, but soon after, Trevor returned to claim his position. Tensions between the band members continued until Kevin, Phil and Keith left, Bruce joined The Clefs (and later Billy Thorpe and the Aztecs), and Trevor formed a new band called Home. It was the end of the band that had recorded *The Happy Prince*.

With Kevin Borich taking the lead, he, Phil Key and Keith Barber took back the band name and reformed with a new bass player. They took on a manager, Michael Chugg, who guided their career for the next few years. (For a detailed description of the band in the later stage of their career see Matheson 1975.) The band remained tied contractually to EMI who required another album from them. Under Borich's musical stewardship, they went back to a bluesy sound. With that line-up they finally cracked the Australian charts in 1971, initially with the Borich penned song 'Gonna See My Baby Tonight' (reaching the top twenty of the *Go Set* charts in early 1972). That was followed with 'Mornin', Good Morning', which was co-written by Borich and Key and showcased Phil's vocals (it reached 24 on *Go Set*'s National charts in March 1972). Still differences in approaches remained and soon after the success of these singles, Key left the band, taking the bass player, Peter Roberts, with him. With another Kiwi, Eddie Hansen, they formed Band of Light in September 1972 and had success in a single, 'Destiny Song', and with their album *Total Union*. Borich held on to the La De Da's name and in 1972 completed obligations to EMI in recording the LP, *Rock And Roll Sandwich* with Rod Coe, once an early fan in Christchurch, now their producer. Initially EMI put Borich and the band into Studio 301. But Borich refused to record there and instead convinced Coe to record them in an abandoned pub. The sound Coe recorded captured the raw energy of this version of the La De Da's and *Rock And Roll Sandwich* has been lauded as a great example of 1970s Australian rock. There was another two years of successful touring but in 1975 the La De Da's were finally disbanded. A reunion to commemorate Eldred Stebbing's Galaxie nightclub was held in 1992 too late for Phil Key, who died in 1984 (he had a congenital heart condition). Trevor, Bruce, Keith Barber and Kevin came back together for one final show that was recorded for video as 'Reunion'.

The Happy Prince is a flawed masterpiece: too close to Oscar Wilde's text to stand out as work of contemporary psychedelic music but too tied into the production and marketing of popular music to find an audience outside a coterie of publicists and supporters. The band itself, while seasoned performers, were still young in 1969 (around twenty-one and twenty-two years old) and headstrong, naively convinced that they did not need to market the album in Australia and New Zealand, but could take on the world with their newly minted vinyl under their arm. The album's potential for success was undermined by the very enthusiasm that sustained it over so many twists and turns. As the music disappeared the myths of its production multiplied. Sydney, Melbourne and Adelaide were reported as sites of its early production. Various labels were identified as being behind the project. In the end, pure luck led to the circumstances whereby the band could record the passion project they had nursed along for nearly two years. Initially a way to open a door to creative song-writing, the band took Oscar Wilde's most audacious and popular fairy tale to heart. Its social critique, championing the 'good act' as an antidote to hypocrisy, underpinned a narrated song cycle that had aspirations to international recognition that were never realized.

Despite its limitations, *The Happy Prince* epitomizes a 1960s critical imagination. Western middle-class values were firmly in its gun sight. The themes – mistrust of progress, money and the moral leadership of society – emerged from city cultures that swirled around the band on its journey from Rutherford High School to EMI's 301 studio. Initiated in Auckland's civic conservatism, punctuated as it was by cultural intensities, *The Happy Prince* was shaped the crass, corrupt commercialism of Sydney and Melbourne's cold decadence. The band absorbed these influences creating space to express them through long improvised performances in East Coast discotheques in Sydney and Melbourne. The band's insistence on doing things their way sustained a creative, critical practice, exemplifying late 1960s musical experimentation, to produce one of the most interesting albums to emerge from Oceania's beat and psychedelic scene.

Notes

Introduction

1 Note on spelling: I use the band's preferred spelling: La De Da's. The apostrophe was most often dropped by reporters and even by record companies. Nevertheless, quotations retain author's spelling.

2 For an excellent online biography of the La De Da's overall career, see Peter Sargent's site https://www.sergent.com.au/music/ladedas.html. Some details in Sargent's account have been corrected in researching this book.

Chapter 1

1 The 'new permissiveness' also led to New Zealand's first lesbian social club, KG Club, opening in 1972, followed by other gay venues'. See Van Beek's (2015) reminiscence.

2 *Billboard* (1967) reported that the song was banned in Australia but there is little to indicate the cause. Occasionally discs were banned for technical reasons but there was also a censorial moral regime within Australian radio. See Rofe (1968), who identifies a number of singles that were banned from radio airplay. (For more on banned songs see the website: **https://bloomsbury.pub/the-happy-prince/banned-songs**).

3   In 2020, The Chicks were inducted into New Zealand music's hall of fame along with Dinah Lee, who was another star in the making in 1960s Auckland.

4   As is often the case a mythology has built up around the name change. It is generally attributed to an intervention of someone's mother (usually Trevor's, sometimes Phil Key's) who was concerned that the names the boys were considering had criminal connotations. Gillanders and Welsh suggested the name change was brought on after the band was renamed The Gonks by a promoter for a gig where a newspaper reporter wrote that Ray Columbus, then the country's most popular singer, described them as 'just another teenage band' (159).

5   As in Britain at the time – but different to Australia as I discuss in a later chapter – there was no commercial radio licence in New Zealand.

6   On the Stebbing's studio and innovation, see Gillanders and Welsh (98–9).

Chapter 2

1   *Film Exercise* (1966) and related notes can be viewed at Ngā Taonga, the audiovisual archive of Aotearoa New Zealand. For an historical discussion of the film's place in early New Zealand cinema, see 'Twenty years of experimental film' (Horrocks 1982). For a general discussion of New Zealand, film and the counterculture, see Bollinger (2022: 145–8).

2   Ted Spring identified the original Yardbirds link with his recollections of attending the recording sessions. That year the Yardbirds – whose songs the La De Da's covered – had

provided soundtrack music and performed in Michelangelo Antonioni's *Blow Up* (1966).

3   Shelly Gane recalled the filmmaking as a formative experience despite the constraints of patriarchal values: 'Nobody filled me in on the script I just did what I was told. Typical of the era I'm afraid. I was the only female at the School of Architecture at the time. During my four years there not one member of the staff had a one-to-one conversation with me! Very disconcerting and confusing!' (personal communication).

4   If there was an antidote to the La De Da's 'Don't You Stand in My Way', it came three years later with The Fourmyula's 'Nature', which has, retrospectively, become a symbolic Aotearoan pop pastoral, an Arcadian integration of the nature and reason: 'Rustling whistling leaves, turning breeze to speech'. Yet Fourmyula never played the song to local audiences in Aotearoa believing that it would not be well received (*New Zealand History*).

5   Grassroots activism in Aotearoa around gay and lesbian rights began in earnest around 1972 after Ngahuia Te Awekotuku, an outspoken lesbian and cultural activist, was denied a permit to visit the United States.

6   The currency of the story continues as, for example, Rupert Everett named his passion project, a film about Oscar Wilde that he produced, directed and starred in, *The Happy Prince* (2018). In 2019, the BBC released a televisual adaptation of Micheál MacLiammóir's one-hander, *The Importance of Being Oscar*.

7   In 1945, Decca released the Welles/Crosby production as a 78 rpm LP with musical direction by Victor Young. Bruce Howard's family also owned the original two record set

of Decca release (thanks to Melanie & Denis Winters, who shared a photograph of the Howard family LPs). In 1949, as vinyl LPs were being established, the Welles/Crosby version of the 'The Happy Prince' was combined with other stories voiced by Crosby, and re-recorded with Lurene Tuttle as the voice of The Swallow and an original musical score composed by Bernard Herrmann. In 1986 John Gielgud also recorded 'The Happy Prince'.

8   After hearing Otis Redding's recording at a friend's place in Auckland, where the cruise docked, Merritt would go on to develop his most successful line-up, with Stewie Spears, Bob Bertles and John 'Yuk' Harrison when he returned to Australia in 1967. With this band he took on a soul-inflected style (McHenry 1996).

Chapter 3

1   For a detailed overview of the Askin government's corruption, see Hickie (1985). There has been debate about the extent of Askin's perfidy, but a more recent article reveals new sources for Hickie's claims (Steketee 2021).

2   Melbourne had a different set of conditions for commercial radio, with the union supported 3KZ having a free flow format that supported a variety of new talent, not just Top 40 acts. This format allowed the dominance of 3KZ dj Stan Rofe in local Melbourne music (see Homan et al. 2021 in particular 'Media City' 73–6). Rofe also became an influential columnist for *Go-Set*.

3   Festival provides a good example of the tangled skeins of influence that underpinned Sydney's networks. Originally

a record manufacturing company, Microgroove, an early merchant banker turned it into a recording label in 1952. Between 1957 and 1961, Festival was owned by real estate magnate L. J. Hooker. Hooker, a fan of pop music, who established his own boutique label, Rex, named after the Sydney hotel that he owned and later a venue for Max Merritt and the Meteors in their cabaret days. In 1961, the company was then sold to the Australian media company, Rupert Murdoch's News Limited, which controlled the company until it was liquidated in 2005 (Milesago 'Record Labels: Festival' n.d.).

Chapter 4

1 Browning was in partnership with Peter Raphael and went onto manage AC/DC as well as work with Michael Gudinski, founder of Mushroom, Australia's premier independent recording and management agency (Milesago, Industry: Michael Browing). The formation of Cordon Bleu came soon after the formation of a new agency in Sydney, NOVA (National Organisation of Variety Artists). For a comprehensive description of Harry Widmer's achievements see his obituary in the *Sydney Morning Herald* (Davis 2002).

2 The liner notes of the 2005 CD release which includes the songs as tracks without narration as well as the original format with Rawlin's contribution.

3 Aulton took Tymepiece into the Festival studio and renamed them The Love Machine to record 'The Lion Sleeps Tonight' (1968), a stunt to mark the opening of an African Lion Safari on Sydney's outskirts in August that year (Towers Interview).

Harris was clearly affected by his time with the band. He told me: 'I'm just a footnote' (Harris Interview).

4   Pastoral Symphony's single, 'The Love Machine', was closely followed by Aulton's Sydney-based studio group that he named The Love Machine (see Note 3 above). It is likely this was Aulton's in-joke, to name his band after Stewart's successful single.

5   On Jolly's role in developing a cultural precinct in Adelaide, see 'Urban Exploration – Derek Jolly's Melbourne Street Futuro House' in Autopsy of Adelaide (2017). The Moog was eventually installed in Gamba in 1969 (*Adelaide Review* 2019; Symons 1969b).

6   This comment is sometimes glossed in later references to the band as 'psychedelic gods'. (See, for example Dix 1988: 70–1; *Milesago* 'Groups and solo artists: La De Das'.)

Chapter 5

1   Popular music was, however, becoming an increasingly important component of consumer sales. Figures for 1968 show that over the previous four years there had been a 50 per cent increase in the production of records in Australia (*The Broadcasting and Television Yearbook* 1968: 144).

2   This trope echoes in later, very different story albums including in Barry Adamson's *Back to the Cat* (2008), where he talks of 'beaten side of town' and Bowie's refrain that 'it happens outside' (*Outside* 1995).

3   Possibly the harshest criticism came twenty years on from the album's release. John Dix (1988) described the album as: 'Puerile and naïve, the inclusion of flute, sitar and choir sits

uneasily with standard rock instrumentation. Adrian Rawlins campy narration is devoid of humour. The project's greatest shortcoming is that it takes itself far too seriously' (p. 71).

4   This is not to discount the strength of the crossover between Beat literature and later rock that Simon Warner (2013) describes in some depth. Despite the closeness between literature and the La De Da's long player, the band tried to sell it as a musical when they were short on opportunities in England in 1969.

5   Bobi Petch (nee Nicholas) recalled that after *The Happy Prince* was released Cordon Bleu secured a well-paying gig for the band, although she could not recall where it was: 'Their last job I got for them was $1000 bucks [sic] for their night [for a] gig, north of Sydney […] That was huge money. [Usually] 50 bucks a week. So, $1000 bucks for the group for the night … I think they all got to London on that.'

Bibliography

Interviews

Ursula Bakker

Kevin Borich

Rodney Charters

Rod Coe

Shelly Gane

Grant Gillanders

Bryan Harris

Dennis and Sonia Key

Brian King

Lonnie Lee

Hugh Lynn

Brett Nielsen

Bobi Petch

Jill Porteous

Jim Stewart

Jim Towers

Geoffrey Weule

Papers – Unpublished

Papers of Adrian Rawlins MSS 252, Special Collections, UNSW Canberra, Australian Defence Force Academy, Canberra, John Howard Reading Room.

- Letter to Gavin [sic] Disney. (1972) 3 July, MSS 252 Correspondence, Box 7, Folder 55.
- Poetry and Jazz 'beat' the rap – a memoir by Adrian Rawlins, unpublished, MSS 252, Box 3, Folder 18.

Oral Histories – Unpublished

Dent G. (1992), Interview, Tape 1–4, Pop Music Oral History Project, OHColl-0485. 24 November, Alexander Turnbull Library, Wellington, New Zealand.

National Library of Australia (NLA) (1994), Rawlins, Adrian and Coleman, Peter, *Adrian Rawlins interviewed by Peter Coleman [sound recording]*. ORAL TRC 3104.

References

Adelaide Review (2019), 'Electric Dreams: Derek Jolly and Australia's First Synthesiser'. No.476. Available online: https://www.adelaidereview.com.au/arts/music/2019/10/22/derek-jolly-moog-synthesiser-australia-adelaide/ (accessed 4 July 2024).

Alexander, L. (1967), 'Discotheques: What's It All about Harold', *Go Set*, 5 July, 10–11.

Auden, W. H. (1963), 'An Improbable Life', *New Yorker*, 39, 9 March, 155–7.

Australian Graphic Design c.1960—>c.1990 'Re:Collection: Frank Eidlitz (1923–1997)'. Biographies. Available online: https://recollection.com.au/biographies/frank-eidlitz (accessed 4 July 2024).

Australian Songwriter (2014), 'Interview: Kevin Borich', 103, August, 12–19. Available online: https://www.asai.org.au/magazine-issue-103/ (accessed 1 July 2024).

Autopsy of Adelaide (2017), 'Urban Exploration – Derek Jolly's Melbourne Street Futuro House'. Available online: https://autopsyofadelaide.com/2017/08/29/derek-jollys-melbourne-street-futuro-house/ (accessed 4 July 2024).

Baigent, G. (1967), *Unseen City*, Blackwood & Janet Paul, Auckland.

Beattie, J. (2014), 'Looking for Arcadia: European Environmental Perception in 1840–1860', *Environment and Nature in NZ*, Vol 9:1. February. Available online: http://www.environmentalhistory-au-nz.org/2014/03/looking-for-arcadia-european-environmental-perception-in-1840-1860/ (accessed 3 July 2024).

Billboard (1967), 'From the Music Capitals of the World, Sydney', 21 October, 48.

Billboard (1968), 'From the Music Capitals of the World, Sydney', 17 February, 45.

Bojic, Z. (2007), *Imaginary Homelands, the Art of Danila Vassilieff*, Andrejevic Endowment, Belgrade.

Bollinger, N. (2022), *Jumping Sundays; The Rise and Fall of the Counterculture in Aotearoa New Zealand*, Auckland University Press, Auckland.

Bourke, C. (2013), 'Never Be Blue', *The Lost Dawn of New Zealand Popular Music*. Available online: https://bluesmokebook. wordpress.com/2013/05/09/never-be-blue/ (accessed 1 July 2024).

Boyd, Winifred J. (2023), 'Historical Qualitative and Quantitative Overview of Classic Literature Embraced by Rock n' Roll, 1960–2000', *SLIS Connecting*, 12, 1. https://doi.org/10.18785/ slis.1201.12

Bracewell, M. (1997), *England Is Mine*, Flamingo, London.

Brown, G. (2018), *Sunshine Secrets; The Story of Ivan Dayman and the Sunshine Record Label*, Moonlight Publishing, Colac.

Caddick, C. (2017), 'The Chicks Part 1 – Down on the Farm', Audioculture, 23 November. Available online: https://www. audioculture.co.nz/articles/the-chicks-part-1-down-on-the-farm (accessed 1 July 2024).

Caddick, C. (2018), 'Ten Moments in New Zealand Prog', Audioculture, 6 December. Available online: https://www. audioculture.co.nz/articles/ten-moments-in-new-zealand-prog (accessed 12 March 2025).

Carr, D. (1962), 'Mushroom growth of urban Auckland', in *Auckland; Expanding to Greatness pub*, Brecknell and Nichols, Auckland, 45–9

Cartwright, G. (2013), 'Queen of the Mods', Audioculture, 20 May. Available online: https://www.audioculture.co.nz/articles/ dinah-lee-queen-of-the-mods (accessed 4 July 2024).

Case, G. (2010), *Out of Our Heads; Rock 'n' Roll before the Drugs Wore Off*, Backbeat Books, Milwaukee.

Charters, R. (1966), *Film Exercise*, Ngā Taonga, the audiovisual archive of Aotearoa New Zealand. Available online: https:// www.ngataonga.org.nz/search-use-collection/search/F23088/ (accessed 2 July 2024).

City of Sydney, Archives & History Resources. Available online: https://archives.cityofsydney.nsw.gov.au/nodes/view/794708 (accessed 17 July 2025).

Cox, P. (2001), *Spinning Around: The Festival Records Story*, Powerhouse Publishing, Sydney.

Davis, T. (2002), 'Many Lives Squeezed into One', *Sydney Morning Herald*, 14 May. Available online: https://www.smh.com.au/national/many-lives-squeezed-into-one-20020514-gdfa09.html (accessed 4 July 2024).

Delia, M. (2024), The Aussie Music Blogspot. Available online: http://theaussiemusicblog.blogspot.com/2014/06/the-la-de-dasfirst-3-albums-1966-1969.html (accessed 28 July 2024).

Dennis, F. (1969), 'Led Zeppelin: *Led Zeppelin* (Atlantic)', *Oz*, March. Retrieved from Rock's Backpages http://www.rocksbackpages.com/Library/Article/led-zeppelini-led-zeppelini-atlantic (accessed 19 February 2025).

de Pont, D. (2021), *New Zealand Swings*, Exhibition essay, Auckland Art Gallery, 20 December. Available online: https://www.aucklandartgallery.com/article/new-zealand-swings?q=%2Farticle%2Fnew-zealand-swings (accessed 3 July 2024).

Dix, J. (1988), 'The ten year saga of the La De Da's', in *Stranded in Paradise New Zealand Rock'n'Roll, 1955–1988*, Paradise Publications, Wellington, 67–75.

Dix, J. (2014a), 'From Pembrokeshire to Paradise', Audioculture, 6 March. Available online: https://www.audioculture.co.nz/articles/john-dix-from-pembrokeshire-to-paradise (accessed 4 July 2024).

Dix, J. (2014b), 'New Zealand Invasion of Australia – the 1960s and Early 1970s', Audioculture, 7 November. Available online: https://www.audioculture.co.nz/articles/new-zealand-invasion-of-australia-the-1960s-and-early-1970s (accessed 4 July 2024).

Edmonds, M. (2021), *Time to Make a Song and Dance; Cultural Revolt in Auckland in the 1960s*, Auckland University Press, Auckland.

Elfick, D. (1969), 'Are the La De Das Happy Prince's', *Go Set*, 26 March, 10.

Elley, D. (2017), 'Rutherford High School, Te Atatu, Auckland – "the Best Thing about Rutherford Was Leaving"'. Available online: https://donaldelley.wordpress.com/2017/05/12/rutherford-high-school-te-atatu-auckland-the-best-thing-about-rutherford-was-leaving/#comments (accessed 1 July 2024).

Forrester (1969), 'A Little Wilde Flower Power' ('TV-Radio Guide', 4) *The Age*, 26 June, 30.

Gambie, G. and Suich, M. (1967), 'We Toured Sydney's Square Mile of Fear', *Sun Herald*, 26 February, 4–5.

Gillanders, G. (2021), *The La De Da's Concept Album The Happy Prince*, Audioculture, 30 July. Available online: https://www.audioculture.co.nz/articles/the-la-de-da-s-concept-album-the-happy-prince (accessed 3 July 2024).

Gillanders, G. and Welsh, R. (2019), *Wired for Sound; The Stebbing History of New Zealand Music*, Bateman Books, Auckland.

Gilmore, Denis 'Speedy' (1995), *A Drummers Story; The More Things Change, the More They Stay the Same*, Moonlight Publications, Golden Square.

Gorman, C. (2010), *Before the Fringe*, Stage Whispers, June. Available online: https://www.stagewhispers.com.au/history/fringe (accessed 4 July 2024).

Go Set (1967a), 'Ginza Discotheque', advertisement, 28 June, 17.

Go Set (1967b), 'North to Coburg', Swingers Nightclub Advertisement, 16 August, 22.

Go Set (1967c), 'Love-In Happens in Carlton', 23 August, 6.

Go Set (1967d), 'Disc Review', 13 September, 2.

Go Set (1967e), 'La De Da's in N.Z.', 20 September, 18.

Go Set (1968), 'La De Da's Go into Seclusion', 27 November, 7.

Go Set (1969) 'Groups Most Likely to Succeed in '69', 1 January, 17.

Grattan, P., 'Peter's Top 10 Star Picks of the 60's and 70's The La De Das', *Memories of New Zealand Musicians*. Archived site. Available online: https://ndhadeliver.natlib.govt.nz/webarchive/20190503081355/http://www.nzmusos.co.nz/ (accessed 2 July 2024).

Green, R. (1965), 'Their Pop-Art Disc Is Like Fly Paper!' Says Who Manager Kit Lambert', *Record Mirror*, 12 June.

Grigg, S. (2018), 'Alan Galbraith'. Audioculture. Available online: https://www.audioculture.co.nz/profile/alan-galbraith (accessed 2 July 2024).

Hickie, D. (1985), *The Prince and the Premier*, Angus and Robertson, Sydney.

Holman, J. P. (2020), *Guest Writer Jeffrey Paparoa Holman Sees a Beat and a Beatle in performance*, Elsewhere, 5 September. Available online: https://www.elsewhere.co.nz/othervoicesotherrooms/9569/guest-writer-jeffrey-paparoa-holman-sees-a-beat-and-a-beatle-in-performance/ (accessed 3 July 2024).

Homan, S., O'Hanlon, S., Strong, C. and Tebbutt, J. (2021), *Melbourne Music City*, Bloomsbury, New York.

Horrocks, R. (1982), 'Twenty Years of Experimental Film', *Art New Zealand*, Issue 24 Winter. Available online: https://art-newzealand.com/24-20years/ (accessed 1 July 2024).

Hoskyns, B. (2003), *Across The Great Divide … The Band & America*, Pimlinco, United Kingdom.

I Am the Platypus, The Beatles in Australia, Sgt. Pepper's Lonely Hearts Club Band General Album Information. Available online: https://www.beatlesaustralia.com/10_PEPPERS_0_overview.html (accessed 4 July 2024).

Ingham, M. (2017), 'Popular song and adaptation', in Thomas Leitch (ed.), *The Oxford Handbook of Adaptation Studies*, Oxford Handbooks, New York, 324–39.

'It's been a nightmare', unidentified news report, in possession of the author.

Jenkins, J. (2023), 'Did the Rock Opera Concept Actually Originate Down Under', *The Music*, 13 July. Available online: https://themusic.com.au/features/did-the-rock-opera-concept-actually-originate-down-under/ROT6VllYW1o/13-08-23 (accessed 2 July 2025).

Jones, J. (2015), *The Executives; Their Aim Was to Please You*, Jaesen Jones.

Kinkead, E. (1957), 'The Study of Something New in History', *The New Yorker*, 26 October, 114.

Laver, J. (1963), *Oscar Wilde*, rev. ed., Longmans, Green & Company for the British Council and National Book League, London.

MacDonald, I. (1995), *Revolution in the Head*, Pimlico, London.

MacInnes, C. (1959), *Absolute Beginners*, Allison and Busby, London.

Marks, I. D. and McIntyre, I. (2010), *Wild about You! The Sixties Beat Explosion in Australia and New Zealand*, Verse Chorus Press, Melbourne.

Matheson, J. (1975), 'The La De Das Story', *Rolling Stone* (Australia), 13 March, 37–40.

McCartney, P. (2017), 'You Gave Me the Answer', Sgt. Pepper Special, Paulmccartney.com. Available online: https://www.paulmccartney.com/news/you-gave-me-the-answer-sgt-pepper-special (accessed 3 July 2024).

McCoy, A. (1980), *Drug Traffic: Narcotics and Organized Crime in Australia*, Harper and Row, Sydney.

McFarlane, I. (1999), 'The Twilights, in *The Encyclopedia of Australian Rock and Pop*, Allen and Unwin, St Leonards, N.S.W, 65–54.

McFarlane, I. (2017), *Our Evolution Just Begun*, Liner notes, 'Evolution' Tamam Shud, Aztec Records.

McHenry, P. (1996), *The Fax about Max; An Overview of the Musical Career of Max Merritt*, Moonlight Publications, Golden Square.

McIntyre, I. (2006), ed. *Tomorrow Is Today: Australia in the Psychedelic Era, 1966–1970*, Wakefield Press, Kent Town.

Meldrum, I. (1968), 'The La De Das, Wandering Minstrels of Pop', *Go Set*, 4 December, 9.

Meldrum, I. (1969a), 'The La De Das; Track by Track', *Go Set*, 2 April, 3.

Meldrum, I. (1969b), 'The La De Das; Side Two, Track by Track', *Go Set*, 9 April, 15.

Meldrum, I. (2016), *Ah Well, Nobody's Perfect; the Untold Stories*, with Jeff Jenkins, Allen and Unwin.

Middleton, R. (1972), 'Way out pop', chapter 12 in *Pop Music and the Blues: A Study of Its Relationship and Significance*, Victor Gollanz, London.

Milesago: Australasian Music & Popular Culture 1964–1975, 'Groups and Solo Artists: La De Das'. Available online: http://www.milesago.com/artists/ladedas.htm (accessed 3 July 2024).

Milesago: Australasian Music & Popular Culture 1964–1975, 'Groups and Solo Artists: Pastoral Symphony'. Available online: http://www.milesago.com/Artists/pastoral.htm (accessed 1 July 2024).

Milesago: *Australasian Music & Popular Culture 1964–1975*, 'Industry: Michael Browning'. Available online: http://www.milesago. com/industry/browning-michael.htm (accessed 4 July 2024).

Milesago: *Australasian Music & Popular Culture 1964–1975*, 'Record Labels: Festival'. Available online: http://www.milesago.com/ industry/festival.htm (accessed 4 July 2024).

Miller, Harry M. (1983), *My Story as Told to Denis O'Brien*, Macmillan, South Melbourne.

Mintrom, C. (2018), 'Kevin Borich: A Fan's Notes', Audioculture. Available online: https://www.audioculture.co.nz/articles/ kevin-borich-a-fan-s-notes (accessed 1 July 2024).

New Zealand History, 'Wayne Mason and the Song "Nature"'. Available online: https://nzhistory.govt.nz/media/photo/ wayne-mason-and-the-song-nature (accessed 1 July 2024).

Nunns, P. (2014), *Robert Ellis's Apocalyptic Vision of Auckland*. Available online: https://www.greaterauckland.org. nz/2014/07/23/robert-elliss-apocalyptic-vision-of-auckland/ (accessed 1 July 2024).

NZOnScreen, *Film Exercise*, Short Film. Available online: https:// www.nzonscreen.com/title/film-exercise-1966 (accessed 1 July 2024).

Organ, M. (2015), 'Yardbirds Australasian Tour 1967' blogspot, 23 May. Available online: https://yardbirdsoz67.blogspot.com/ (accessed 13vMarch 2025).

Organ, M. (2019), 'The World's First Psychedelic Jazz Concert – Psychedelia, Sydney, 1967', *Counterculture Studies*, 2, 1, 43–73. DOI:10.14453/ccs.v2.i1.14.

Patterson, L. (1967), 'La De Da's Invade Australia', *The Sun-Herald*, 21 May, 98.

Raban, J. (1988), 'The soft city', in *Soft City*, Collins Harvill, London, 9–16

Rae, C. (2020), *William S. Burroughs and the Cult of Rock'n'roll*, White Rabbit Books, London.

Rawlins, A. (1966a), 'Ten Statements re Bob Dylan [with a postscript]', (TV-Radio Guide 4.) *The Age*, 27 January, 26.

Rawlins, A. (1966b), 'Bob Dylan and the Now Mind Situation', *Arena*, 10, 4, 24–8.

Rawlins, A. (1969), 'New Voices Tell Old Story' (Sound and Recording Supplement, 7) *The Age*, 17 April, 35.

Rawlins, A. (1994), *Dylan: Through the Looking Glass*, All Night Cafe, Carlton.

Reekie, T. (2014), 'Moments Like These: Kevin Borich', *NZMusician*, April/May. Available online: https://nzmusician.co.nz/features/kevin-borich/ (accessed 1 July 2024).

Riley, J. (2019), *The Bad Trip; Dark Omens, New Worlds and the End of the Sixties*, Icon Books, London.

Robinson, D. M. (1962), *Auckland; Expanding to Greatness*, ed. Fred C. Symes, pub. Brecknell and Nichols, Auckland, 40–4.

Rofe, S. (1967), 'Stan Rofe's Tonic', *Go Set*, 19 July, 3.

Rofe, S. (1968), 'The Shocking Songs; A D.J. Tells the Inside Story of Restricted Airplay', *Go Set*, 28 August, 17.

Rutherford Yearbook (1963), 'A New Softness', editorial, Vol.1:3 December, 3. Available online: https://www.rutherford.school.nz/our-community/alumni/alumni-yearbooks (accessed 1 July 2024).

Selvin, J. (1995), *Summer of Love; The Inside Story of LSD, Rock & Roll, Free Love and High Times in the Wild West*, Plume Books, New York.

Sergent, B., 'La De Da's', *New Zealand Music of the 50's, 60's, 70's and a Bit of 80's* Artists L – Z. Available online: https://www.sergent.com.au/music/ladedas.html (accessed 1 July 2024).

Shadowplay, 'In Search of Visions, Nevill Drury Interview'. Available online: http://www.shadowplayzine.com/Interviews/nevill_interview.htm (accessed 4 July 2024).

Sovatsky, S. (2004), 'Clinical Forms of Love Inspired by Meher Baba's Mast Work and the Awe of Infinite Consciousness', *The Journal of Transpersonal Psychology*, 36, 2.

Stanfield, P. (2017), 'The Who and Pop Art: The Simple Things You See Are All Complicated', *Journal of Popular Music Studies*, 29, 1. DOI: 10.1111/jpms.12203.

Stead, C. K. (1992), 'A Kiwi remembers,' in Barry Humphries, *More Please: An Autobiography*, Viking, London, 325–26

Steketee, M. (2021), 'Was Bob Askin Corrupt?', *Inside Story*, 9 April. Available online: https://insidestory.org.au/was-bob-askin-corrupt/ (accessed 1 July 2024).

Stephens, J. (1998), *Anti-disciplinary Protest; Sixties Radicalism and Postmodernism*, Cambridge University Press, Cambridge.

Sun-Herald (1967a), 'La De Da's Invade Aust', 21 May, 98.

Sun Herald (1967b), 'Total Sound You Can See … ', 3 September, 104.

Sun-Herald (1968a), 'Three Groups Get a Touch of Efficiency', 4 February, 89.

Sun Herald (1968b), 'Young World, What's On', 5 May, 59.

Sun-Herald (1968c), 'Glitter', 27 October, 103.

Sydney Mail (1928), 'Prince Edward Theatre', 28 November, 22. Available online: http://nla.gov.au/nla.news-article158403560 (accessed 6 March 2025).

Sydney Morning Herald (1967), 'Holt in Close-up/Growl', 8 July, 12.

Sydney Morning Herald (1970), 'The Acid Test', advertisement, 3 July, 19.

Sydney Morning Herald (1976), 'This Apan Is a Good Solid Family Turntable', advertisement, 9 December, 28.

Sydney Morning Herald (1980), 'Listen and You Will Hear Why Professionals Get so Excited about Sony', advertisement, 30 November, 16.

Symons, M. (1969a), 'Sweet Peach Has a Good Look', *Sydney Morning Herald*, 27 September, 9.

Symons, M. (1969b), 'Moog Hat at Sweet Peach', *Sydney Morning Herald*, 10 May, 15.

The Age (1967), 'Compere Hit on Drug "Trip"', 7 July, 3.

The Broadcasting and Television Yearbook (1968), Greater Publications, Sydney.

The Bulletin (1967), 'Psychedelic Underpants Give a Man Assurance', Batman's Melbourne, 1 July, 5.

'The Grant Gillanders Collections' (2016), 'For the Love of It', Elsewhere. Available online: https://www.elsewhere.co.nz/somethingelsewhere/7503/the-grant-gillanders-collections-2016-for-the-love-of-it/ (accessed 1 July 2024).

The Happy Prince (2005), CD liner notes. EMI Music New Zealand.

The Press (1960), 'Oscar Wilde', Savoy Theatre Advertisement, 1. Available online: https://paperspast.natlib.govt.nz/newspapers/press/1960/07/06/1 (accessed 3 July 2024).

The Press (1963), 'The Man with the Green Carnation' Avon Theatre advertisement, 4 May, Column 4, 1. Available online: https://paperspast.natlib.govt.nz/newspapers/CHP19630504.2.5.4 (accessed 3 July 2024).

The Press (1964a), 'The Man with the Green Carnation', Hollywood Theatre advertisement, 15 December, Column 10, 29. Available online: https://paperspast.natlib.govt.nz/newspapers/CHP19641215.2.235.10 (accessed 3 July 2024).

The Press (1964b), 'Wilde's Personality in One– Man Show', 29 June, 14.

The Treatment (2022), 'The Treat: Director George Miller on Oscar Wilde's "The Happy Prince"', Radio KCRW Feature, 1 October. Available online: https://www.kcrw.com/culture/shows/the-treatment/director-tyler-perry-director-walter-hill-and-the-treat-a-childhood-favorite-with-george-miller/george-miller-oscar-wilde-happy-prince (accessed 3 July 2024).

Thoms, A. (2000), 'Evolution', chapter 8, *Surfmovies; The History of Surf Films in Australia*, Shorething Publishing, Noosa Heads, Qld, 93–108.

Tomkins, C. (1965), 'In the Outlaw Area', *The New Yorker*, 31 December. Available online: https://www.newyorker.com/magazine/1966/01/08/in-the-outlaw-area (accessed 1 July 2024).

Unseen City (2015), Exhibition Notes, City Gallery, Wellington. Available online: https://citygallery.org.nz/exhibitions/unseen-city/ (accessed 1 July 2024).

Van Beek, K. (2015), 'Kathryn Van Beek Pays Tribute to Auckland's Shady Lady', Elsewhere, 19 October. Available online: https://www.elsewhere.co.nz/othervoicesotherrooms/7212/guest-writer-kathyrn-van-beek-pays-tribute-to-aucklands-shady-lady/ (accessed 1 July 2024).

Veitch, J. (1969), 'Pop Time with Jock Veitch', *Sun Herald*, 8 June, 77.

Warburton, N. (2009), *The Wild Cherries*, garagehangover. Available online: https://garagehangover.com/wildcherries/ (accessed 4 July 2024).

Warner, S. (2013), *Text and Drugs and Rock'n'Roll; the Beats and Rock Culture*, Bloomsbury, New York.

Watkins, P. (1995), *Hostage to the Beat*, Tanden Press, Birkenhead.

Welch, C. (1966), 'The Who: A Quick One (Reaction)', *Melody Maker* 10 December.

Wood, N. (2002), 'Creating the Sensual Child; Paterian Aesthetics, Pederasty, and Oscar Wilde's Fairy Tales', *Marvels and Tales*, 16, 2, 156–70.

Wrokdown (2016), 'Mary Renshaw and Howard Gable', interviewed by Wendy Stapleton, Gable quote at: 29'39", 11 July. Available online: https://www.youtube.com/watch?v=a95_j1eXrYE (accessed 4 July 2024).

Discography

LPs

Adamson, Barry (2008) *Back to the Cat*, Central Control International.

Ashdown, Doug (1970) *The Age of Mouse*, Sweet Peach.

Band of Light (1973) *Total Union*, Warner Bros. Records, CD rerelease (2006) Aztec Records.

The Beatles, (1967) *Sergeant Pepper's Lonely Hearts Club*, EMI.

The Beatles, (1969) *Abbey Road*, EMI.

Bowie, David (1995) *Outside*, RCA.

Cream (1968) *Disreali Gears*, Reaction.

Deep Purple (1968) *The Book of Taliesyn*, Tetragrammaton Records.

The Fifth Dimension (1967) *The Magic Garden*, Liberty.

La De Da's (1966) The *La De Da's*, Phillips, New Zealand.

La De Da's (1967) *Find Us a Way*, Phillips, New Zealand.

La De Da's (1969) *The Happy Prince*, Columbia.

La De Da's (2005) *The Happy Prince*, CD release. EMI Music New Zealand.

The Pleazers, (1966) *Definitely Pleazers*, Zodiac Records.

Small Faces (1968) *Ogdens' Nut Gone Flake*, Immediate.

Tamam Shud (1969, 2018) *Evolution*, CD rerelease, Aztec Records.

Traffic (1967) *Mr Fantasy*, Island.

The Twilights (1968) *Once upon a Twilight*, EMI.

Vanilla Fudge (1967) *Vanilla Fudge*, Atco.

The Who (1966) *A Quick One*, Polydor.

The Who (1969) *Tommy*, Polydor.

Singles

The Beatles, (1963) 'I Want to Hold Your Hand', Parlaphone.

Booker T and the MG's, (1962) 'Green Onions' / 'Behave Yourself', Stax.

Columbus, Ray and the Invaders, (1964) 'She's a Mod', Zodiac.

Dinah Lee, (1965) 'What You Know Yokomo', HMV.

Ebony, (1972) 'Big Norm', Polydor.

The Fourmyula, (1969), 'Nature' / 'Home', His Master's Voice.

The Love Machine, (1968) 'The Lion Sleeps Tonight', Festival.

Pastoral Symphony, (1968) 'The Love Machine', Festival.

The Twilights, (1968) 'Bad Boy', EMI.

The Who, (1965) 'Anyway, Anyhow, Anywhere' / 'Daddy Rolling Stone', Brunswick.

The Yardbirds, (1965) 'Evil Hearted You' / 'Still I'm Sad', Columbia.

Filmography

Blow Up (1966), Dir. Michael Antonioni, England, Metro-Goldwyn-Mayer/Premier Productions.

Film Exercise (1966), Dir. Rodney Charters, New Zealand.

Oscar Wilde (1960), Dir. Gregory Ratoff, England, 20th Century Fox.

Rock around the Clock (1956), Dir. Fred F. Sears, Columbia Pictures, USA.

Snow (1963), Dir. Geoffrey Jones England, British Transport Films.

The Good, the Bad and the Ugly (1967), Dir. Sergio Leone, Spain, United Artists.

The Happy Prince (2018), Dir. Rupert Everett, England BBC Films/Lions Gate UK.

The Trials of Oscar Wilde (1960), also released as *The Man with the Green Carnation*, Dir. Ken Hughes England, United Artists.

Index